A Time with Our Children
Year A

A Time with Our Children
Stories for Use in Worship

Year A

Dianne E. Deming

The Pilgrim Press
Cleveland, Ohio

The Pilgrim Press, Cleveland, Ohio 44115
© 1992 by Dianne E. Deming

Biblical quotations, unless otherwise noted, are from the New Revised Standard Version of the Bible, (c) 1989 by the Division of Christian Education of the National Council of the Churches of Christ in the U.S.A., and are used by permission. Quotations noted NEB are from the New English Bible, (c) by the Delegates of the Oxford University Press and the Syndics of the Cambridge University Press 1961, 1970

Illustrations by Carin Shamley

Printed in the United States of America
The paper used in this publication is acid free and meets the minimum requirements of American National Standard for Information Sciences-Permanence of Paper for Printed Library Materials, ANSI Z39.48-1984

97 96 95 94 93 92   5 4 3 2 1

Library of Congress Cataloging-in-Publication Data

Deming, Dianne E.
    A time with our children : stories for use in worship / Dianne E. Deming.
        p.   cm.
    Includes indexes.
    Contents: [1] Year A
    ISBN 0–8298–0941–4 (year A : alk. paper)
    1. Children's sermons. 2. Church year sermons. I. Title.
BV4315.D422   1992
252'.53—dc20   92–31638
                                                        CIP

For Frank, Scott, and John
With Love

Contents

Acknowledgments

This book came into being only by the grace of God and with the help and support of many people, some of whom I would like to acknowledge here.

Many thanks to my husband, Frank, for his encouragement, love, and practical help at home as the deadline drew near. Many thanks for their support to my parents, Leonard and Anne Jones; to my sister and her husband, Kathy and Dennis Onnen; to my grandfather, A. W. Jones; and to my in-laws, Frank and Carolyn Deming. A special thanks goes to my mom for typing the manuscript.

Thanks to Walter Umla for arranging and writing out the song "Jesus Is the Light of the World," to Carin Shanley for her illustrations, and to the Rev. Lucinda Stafford-Lewis for permission to use her story idea. Thanks to Barbara Withers, Richard Brown, James Heaney, and everyone else at The Pilgrim Press.

Finally, I could not have written this book without the help of the children in my life. Thanks to all of them, especially Scott and John, for helping me remember what it's like to be a child.

Introduction

The children's sermon is a time in worship laden with potential—potential for meaningful experience for both children and adults, as well as potential for disaster.

Parents may worry about being humiliated in front of the congregation by what their children might do or say. What if Jimmy picks a fight with the child sitting next to him on the chancel steps again? What if Susie tells the minister what we said about the church at the supper table last night? Pastors may worry about the prop not working the way it should or about not having any children show up.

These potential problems are obvious and can be dealt with easily enough. What concerns me more is the disaster of missed opportunity that occurs when we fail to make the children's story a time with and for the children. If we use the children's storytime as another chance to make a point with the adults, or as entertainment for the grown-ups' benefit, if we set our children up to be embarrassed or simply don't consider whether or not they know what we're talking about, then we have failed our mission and God's children.

On the other hand, if we view the children's sermon as an opportunity to share our faith with the next generation of believers, if we try to see the world from the children's point of view and address their questions and concerns in words and images they can understand, if we are as open and honest with them as we can be, if we demonstrate God's love by loving the children ourselves, then this time can be a wonderful worship experience for both the children and the adults of the congregation.

The stories in this book are written in an attempt to help you fulfill the positive potential of a time with your children each week. May God bless and be with you in this vital ministry.

How to Use This Book

These stories are written to be helpful to you. Feel free to adapt or change them in any way that would make their telling more effective. Use your own words. Add your own anecdotes or examples. Take these stories and make them your own.

The stories are based on the *Common Lectionary,* Year A. They are indexed in the back of the book both by subject and by Scripture reference for those who do not follow the lectionary.

Several stories call for the use of a flannel board and flannelboard figures. In the Appendix at the back of the book, you will find patterns for the figures and instructions on how to assemble them and the flannel board.

Season of Advent

Happy New Year!

Props Needed
A party hat
A noisemaker
A secular calendar, preferably showing the whole year on one page
An Advent calendar

The Message
(*Wear the party hat.*) Happy New Year, everybody! (*Blow on the horn.*) Did you know that today is the first day of a brand new year? You didn't? Well, let's check the calendar. (*Hold up secular calendar.*) Can any of you find today's date on the calendar for us? (*Choose a volunteer. If there are none, help the group find the date.*) Good! This block of numbers represents the month of November. Today is Sunday, November twenty-ninth. So here is today's date. Let's circle it. (*Draw a circle around the date.*)

Hey wait a minute! If today is the first day of the new year, why are all of these numbers and months on the calendar before today's date? Calendars usually *begin* with the first day of the year, don't they? Which means that today's date should be up here at the top. On what date do we usually think of the new year as starting? (*Pause for answers.*) January first! And today is only November twenty-ninth. But I *know* that today is the first day of the new year. Does anybody have any idea what's going on here? It sure is confusing, isn't it?

Wait a minute. *Now* I remember! Today is the first day of the Christian year, or the church year. The regular year is divided up into months—January, February, March, April, and so on—and into seasons—fall, winter, spring, and summer. The church year is divided up into seasons as well, but the seasons of the church year are not based on the weather or the way plants grow. The church year is based on things that happened in the life of Jesus and the history of the church.

The church year begins with the season of Advent, which starts the fourth Sunday before Christmas and lasts until Christmas Eve. Let's look at our calendar again. Who knows what date Christmas is? (*Pause for answers.*) December twenty-fifth. Right. Here is December twenty-fifth on the calendar. This year Christmas falls on a Friday. Now we need to count back four Sundays from Christmas. All of the numbers in this row on the calendar are Sundays. So let's count together. (*Point to Sundays as you go.*) One, two, three . . . We're out of Sundays in December, so we have to skip back to November and find the fourth Sunday before Christmas. There it is! It's the date we circled earlier, isn't it. Today is the fourth Sunday before Christmas, or the first Sunday in Advent. So, today is the first day of the new church year.

Advent is a fun season in the church year. The word *advent* comes from a Latin word meaning 'arrival' or 'coming.' During the season of Advent, all Christians everywhere get ready for Jesus' birth in Bethlehem. We prepare our hearts and our minds to welcome Jesus into our lives today. And we also look forward to a time when Jesus will come again and rule the world. We'll be talking more about these three different sides of Advent in the next three weeks.

I have one more calendar I want to show you. One way we can celebrate Advent and get ready for Jesus is with the help of an Advent calendar. (*Show the Advent calendar.*) Even though today is the first day of Advent, this calendar doesn't start until December first, which is next Tuesday. On December first, you open the little window with the number one on it. Can you find the number one on the calendar? (*Let the children find the correct window.*) There it is! We'll go ahead and open it, and see what's inside, since we won't be together on Tuesday. It says (or *It's a picture of*). . . Each day, from December first through December twenty-fourth, Christmas Eve, you open a different window. Then, when all the windows are open, you know the next day is Christmas. An Advent calendar can remind us every day to pray, to remember Jesus, and to get ready for Jesus' coming into our world.

So, once again, Happy New Year and Happy Advent to all of you.

Let's Pray. Dear God, we thank you for being with us in our world in new ways all the time. Help us to be ready to receive Jesus' help and love in our loves. Amen.

Isaiah 11:1–10

The Lion and the Mouse

Props Needed

A piece of heavy rope, as might be used in a net to trap a lion

You may want to secure an illustrated version of Aesop's Fable, "The Lion and the Mouse," reading this portion of the message and sharing the pictures with the children

The Message

This morning I want to tell you a fable. A fable is a make-believe story that teaches a moral or a lesson. Most of the time the characters in the story are animals who talk and act like people. This fable was first told years ago by a man named Aesop. It's called "The Lion and the Mouse."

One day a mouse was running through the grassy field where she lived. As she raced toward her hole, she happened to run across the front paws of a sleeping lion. The lion awoke with a grunt, and angrily snatched up the pesky mouse. "How dare you interrupt my rest!" roared the lion. "For that, you shall surely die!" The lion was bringing the tiny mouse to his mouth when he heard her squeak, "Please, Your Majesty, do not eat me. I am so small, you won't even taste me before I'm gone. And besides, if you spare my life, there might be a day when I can help you. You never know."

This idea made the lion roar with laughter. He thought the mouse was so funny—suggesting that such a small creature could someday help a huge beast such as himself—that he let her go. She wasted no time in scurrying down her hole.

Time passed. One day the lion was in the mouse's field again, hunting for food. Before he knew what had happened, he was hanging from a tree, caught in a hunter's net. The net was made of thick rope, like this. (*Show the rope.*) The more the lion struggled to free himself, the more tangled in the rope he became. He let out a mighty, miserable roar.

The mouse, who was nearby, heard the lion's cry and came to his rescue. With her sharp teeth, she gnawed and chewed at the ropes that held the lion, and before long the lion escaped to freedom.

Aesop's moral for this fable is: 'Don't judge a person, or a friend, by his or her size.' But there is another lesson I would like to draw from this story.

God promises us a time when the whole world will be at peace. There will be no wars and no fighting, not even arguments. Everyone will get along, and people will treat each other fairly. Even the animals will be friends. Animals who usually kill and eat each other—wolves and sheep, leopards and goats, even lions and mice—will live together in peace.

This place will be called 'The Realm of God,' and it will be so special because the whole world will finally live as God wants us to live. God will send a special ruler to lead the people in this peaceable realm. That ruler will be Jesus.

People have been waiting for God's Realm for thousands of years. No one knows exactly when or how God will set it up, but looking forward to that time of peace, love, and fairness is one of the things we do during Advent. We can get ready for God's Realm by being the very best people we can be. We can help God by being fair and kind and generous to other people. If you disagree with someone, try to see things from his or her side. And remember that each person, no matter how big or how small, can do something good for others.

Let's Pray. Dear God, we thank you for your many promises to us. In this Advent season, we look forward with hope and anticipation to the fulfillment of your Realm. In Jesus' name. Amen.

THIRD SUNDAY IN ADVENT
Matthew 11:2–11

Good Deeds as
Advent Preparation

In the Spirit
of Nicholas

Prop Needed
A small drawstring pouch filled with gold foil-wrapped chocolate coins

The Message
This morning I want to tell you a story about a special man who lived a long time ago, about three hundred years after Jesus. His name was Nicholas, and he lived in a country called Myra on the other side of the world.

Nicholas was a good man, and he loved Jesus very much. He told everybody about how Jesus showed the world God's love. Many people who heard Nicholas preach believed and became Christians themselves.

Nicholas lived at a time when it wasn't safe to serve the Lord. The emperor of Myra didn't like Christians, and when he heard about Nicholas and his preaching, he threw Nicholas in prison. Nicholas's friends in Myra were sad and afraid.

But God did not forget Nicholas or his friends. A new person named Constantine became emperor. He freed Nicholas from jail and sent him home. Nicholas became the bishop of Myra, and was in charge of all the churches there.

There were three sisters in Myra who were in love and wanted to get married. But these three young women came from a poor family. In those days, the father of a bride had to pay her groom what was called a 'dowry' when the couple was married. The father of these three sisters didn't have enough money for his daughters' dowries, so they couldn't marry the men they loved. The father couldn't even afford to keep the girls himself anymore, and he planned to sell them into a kind of slavery.

Bishop Nicholas heard about the sisters and was worried about them. Late one night, when he thought no one would see him, Nicholas went to the poor family's home. He quietly tossed three

6

bags full of shiny gold coins down the chimney. The bags may have looked something like this. (*Show your drawstring bag.*) When the girls woke up in the morning, they found the bags of coins in the socks they had hung to dry by the chimney. They had their dowries, and that made them very happy, but they were also curious. Where had the money come from? A neighbor had seen the bishop and told the girls that they had Nicholas to thank for saving them from slavery.

So the girls went to see Nicholas, but when they thanked him, he refused to take any credit for his kind deed. He said, "Please do not thank me, but thank god, who gives all good gifts."

Nicholas continued to help the poor. He gave food or clothing to children in need, but he never took credit or bragged about what he did. He always gave the credit to God, the giver of every good gift.

The story of Bishop Nicholas and his kind deeds spread to many lands. Christians all over the world admired Nicholas's strong faith and tried to be like him. When they gave gifts to the poor, they said, "This gift came from Nicholas," rather than taking the credit themselves.

Doing kind things for others is one way we get ready for Jesus' coming into our world at Christmas. There are many chances to give of ourselves during the Advent season. You could bring canned food to the church to help stock the food pantry. This food is given to people who don't have enough to eat. You could shovel a snowy walk or share home-baked cookies with an elderly neighbor, or you could go Christmas caroling at a nursing home this afternoon with others from our church. (*Mention any church or community programs in which the children are able to participate.*)

When we do kind things for others, it is important to remember the lesson Bishop Nicholas teaches us. If we brag about the good we do, or if we do it expecting some sort of reward, our deeds are not as good as they could be. Expecting something in return for kindness somehow ruins the whole thing. Rather, do kind acts in the spirit of Bishop Nicholas, giving all the credit to God, who gives all good gifts.

Let's Pray. Gracious God, we know that every good gift comes from you. Help us to share what we have been given in the unselfish spirit of Nicholas. Amen.

(*You may want to give the children each a candy coin as they leave, and wish them a Merry Christmas in the spirit of Bishop Nicholas.*)

Matthew 1:18–25
Luke 2:1–20

O Holy Night

Props Needed
 A nativity scene with as many pieces as possible
 A flat surface on which to place the crèche (where the figures won't tip over)

The Message
 Well, the waiting's almost over, and Christmas is almost here, isn't it? What have you done during this Advent season to get ready for Christmas? (*Listen to children's answers.*) There is one more thing I would like all of us to do to get ready for Christmas, and that is to tell the Christmas story. Would you like to help me?

 I have little figures of the people and animals that we need to tell the story. I will pass out these pieces to those who would like to help me. When I come to the part of the story that mentions your figure, then you set it up in the stable. (*Pass out the figures. You may want to borrow animals from several different sets or pass out straw for the stable floor so that each child can contribute.*)

 Well, the story really begins before the night Jesus was born. There was a young woman named Mary, and Mary was engaged to Joseph. Mary and Joseph were both looking forward to their wedding. Then one day, God sent the angel Gabriel with a message for Mary, and Gabriel told her that she was going to have a baby. This news frightened Mary because she wasn't married yet, and she didn't know what Joseph would say. But Gabriel told her not to be afraid. God had chosen her to be the mother of a very special baby, and everything would be all right.

 The angel was right. Joseph and Mary started to get ready for the baby's arrival. But before the baby was born, Mary and Joseph had to travel from their home in Nazareth to another town called Bethlehem. The government was taking a census, counting all the people in the realm. Joseph and Mary had to walk to Bethlehem where Joseph's family came from, to be counted.

Bethlehem is about seventy miles from Nazareth, where Mary and Joseph lived. Today, in a car, the trip wouldn't be too bad, It would take a little over an hour, like going from here to _____. (*Mention a place seventy miles from your home.*) But Mary and Joseph didn't have a car. They had to walk the seventy miles from Nazareth to Bethlehem. The trip was especially hard because Mary was due to have her baby at any time.

When they finally got to Bethlehem, every hotel room in town was taken, so they had to spend the night in a stable. (*Set up the stable.*)

Who can tell me what a stable is? (*Pause for answers.*) That's right. A stable is a building where animals are kept. There is usually straw on the floor. Who has straw to put in our stable? (*Have children with straw add it to the floor of the stable.*) The Bible doesn't tell us exactly which animals were in the stable in Bethlehem, but there may have been a donkey. Who has the donkey? Would you like to put him in the stable, Scott? (*Have children put their animals in the stable as you name each one.*)

A stable usually has tools and supplies in it too. We know the stable Mary and Joseph stayed in had a manger. A manger is where oats are put for the animals to eat. Who has our manger?

The animals welcomed Mary and Joseph into their home. (*Place Joseph and Mary figures in stable.*) That night, the baby was born, and they named him Jesus, as the angel had told them to. They wrapped him up to keep him warm and put him in the manger. (*Place Jesus in manger.*)

There were shepherds out in the field that night, taking care of their sheep. God sent an angel to the shepherds to tell them about Jesus' birth. Soon the whole sky was filled with angels singing, "Glory to God in the highest, and on earth, peace."

The shepherds went to the stable to see the new baby. (*Add shepherds and sheep.*) They told Mary and Joseph about the angels, and everyone was amazed.

We are still amazed the God loves us enough to have sent Jesus into the world. Jesus came to show the world God's love, starting out in a stable so many years ago. Jesus is still with us, teaching us of God's amazing love. I hope each of you has a very merry and blessed Christmas as you celebrate Jesus' birth and the miracle of God's love.

Let's Pray. All-loving God, we give you thanks and praise for the blessing that is ours in Christmas. May all people everywhere know your love this season and always. In Jesus' name. Amen.

Season of Christmas

Heavenly Angels and Earthbound Shepherds

Props Needed

A shepherd figure carrying a staff (from last week's crèche; if your figure has no staff, use a picture of one, or perhaps your church has a shepherd's staff with its Christmas pageant costumes)

One candy cane

A candy cane for each child (optional)

The Message

Merry Christmas, everyone! Tomorrow is the big day, isn't it? Last Sunday we told the story of Jesus' birth using the crèche. Now I'm going to test your memory. Who were the first people to be told the news that a very special baby had been born in Bethlehem? (*Pause for answers.*)

The shepherds, that's right! Who delivered the message to the shepherds? (*Pause.*) An angel of the Lord. He appeared to the shepherds while they were out in the field watching over their sheep at night. The angel said, "Don't be afraid. I am bringing you good news of great joy for all the people. Today in David's town your Savior was born—Christ the Lord" (Luke 2:10b-11).

What is a shepherd? Can anybody tell me? (*Listen to answers.*) A shepherd is a person who takes care of flocks of sheep or goats. The shepherd leads the flock to water and grassy fields, so they have enough to drink and eat. Shepherds protect the animals from being eaten by coyotes or stolen by thieves. And if a sheep wanders off and gets lost, the shepherd searches for it and brings it safely back to the flock.

Sometimes a sheep might wander down some rocks and not be able to climb back up to the pasture. This must happen often, because shepherds carry a special tool to help get the sheep out of these tight situations. The tool is called a staff. (*Show your prop.*)

The shepherd from our nativity scene is holding a staff. If a sheep was caught down in some rocks, the shepherd could hook the curved part of the staff under the sheep's front legs and pull it up to safety.

Shepherds were common, ordinary people. They didn't have a lot of money. In fact, compared to many people, they were poor. Some shepherds were children. God chose shepherds to be the first people to hear the good news of Jesus' birth because God wanted common, ordinary people everywhere to know that Jesus was sent into the world for them. God sent Jesus to be the special friend and savior of ordinary people like the shepherds and you and me.

There is a treat that you see every Christmas that can remind you of the shepherds. (*Show a candy cane.*) How might this candy cane remind you of the first people to hear of Jesus' arrival in the stable in Bethlehem? (*Pause for answers.*) It looks like the shepherd's staff, doesn't it? It's shaped like the tool used by the shepherds to rescue lambs and sheep from rocky places. From now on, when you see a candy cane, remember the shepherds and the part they play in the Christmas story. Remember that Jesus was sent by God to rescue common, ordinary people—people like shepherds and people like us—from our sin. Jesus was sent to be our Savior and our special friend.

Let's Pray. Dear God, thank you for the shepherds and the angels and your loving care for all of us. In Jesus' name. Amen.

(*You may want to give the children candy canes as they leave.*)

Moving to Safety

Prop Needed
If your church or community sponsors a refugee family, have a photo of the family

The Message
Good morning, girls and boys. How are all of you this morning? Did you sleep well last night? Did any of you dream dreams while you slept?

Does everybody know what a dream is? A dream is like a story that you think up while you're asleep. Sometimes a dream makes sense, and sometimes it seems as if the story is all mixed up. Sometimes dreams are happy, and sometimes they are sad or scary. Does your dad or mom wish you "sweet dreams" when you're tucked in bed, ready to go to sleep? That means he or she wants you to have happy dreams.

Let's return to Bethlehem, where Jesus was born. It was almost time for Joseph, Mary, and their new baby to leave the stable. They were going home to Nazareth, where Joseph worked as a carpenter. Then one night Joseph had a dream, and in his dream an angel of the Lord spoke to him. That angel told Joseph that it wasn't safe for them to return to Nazareth. Herod, the king, had heard about Jesus' birth, and some people were saying that when Jesus grew up he would take Herod's place as king of Judah. Herod was jealous. He wanted to find the baby Jesus and kill him so he would never be able to take the throne away. The angel told Joseph not to take his family to Nazareth, but rather to escape to Egypt where they would be safe.

When Joseph woke up from his dreams, it was still the middle of the night. He woke Mary and told her what the angel had said. Together they packed up the few things they had with them, bundled up the baby, and quietly left the stable. Joseph took his little family to Egypt, where they could be safe from the angry and jealous King Herod.

They lived in Egypt for a few years. Then the angel appeared to Joseph in another dream. This time the angel said, "Herod is dead. You may go home now." So Joseph, Mary, and Jesus went home to Nazareth where Jesus grew up.

When Joseph, Mary, and Jesus lived in Egypt, they were what we call 'refugees.' Refugees are people who are forced to leave their comes because it isn't safe for them to live there any more. There are many reasons why people might be refugees.

Sometimes people have to leave their homes because their neighborhood has been destroyed by a flood, an earthquake, or a fire. Bad storms like hurricanes or tornadoes can force people to leave their homes and become refugees. During a war, the people who live where the fighting is going on have to leave because their homes are no longer safe. In some countries, if people speak out and complain about or criticize the government, they could be arrested, thrown in jail, tortured, or even killed. If they decide to leave their country in order to save their lives, they are political refugees. Religious refugees are people forced to leave their homes because, in their country, they are not allowed to believe in what they choose to believe about God.

Where do refugees go when they leave home? Sometimes they go to a shelter nearby. If a fire were to destroy several blocks of homes in our town, the Red Cross would set up places for people to sleep at the high school until they could find another place to stay. In times of war, when many, many people have to leave their homes, they sometimes live in camps until the war is over, and it is safe to go home again. If people are in trouble with their government and their whole country is a dangerous place to be, then they try to move to a new country. That is what Joseph, Mary, and Jesus did.

Many refugees come to our country, the United States. They know that here people are free to believe and say what they want, even if it's against the government. We don't have to agree with everything our president says. We are also free to practice any religion we choose. (*If your church sponsors a refugee family, mention them here and show photo.*) I think being a refugee would be scary, don't you? For refugees forced to move to a new country like the United States, things would be very different from home. Many times they don't even know our language when they get here. Imagine how hard it would be, even just going to the grocery store, if you couldn't understand anybody and no one could understand you.

Whenever people move to a new home, it's kind of scary, whether they choose to move or are forced to move like refugees. We can try and make the change easier by being friendly to new people in our neighborhoods, our schools, and our church. By being their friends, we can help newcomers fulfill their dreams of a better life.

Let's Pray. Dear God, we thank you for the freedoms we enjoy in our country. Help us to be friends with new neighbors. Amen.

Epiphany and the Season Following

Matthew 2:1–12

To Be Truly Wise

Props Needed
Flannel board
Flannel-board figures (found in the Appendix)
Many small star stickers

The Message
We've talked a lot about Jesus' birth in the past few weeks, haven't we? We've talked about Joseph and Mary and the baby Jesus, about the stable where Jesus was born, and all the animals that were there. We've mentioned angels and shepherds. But there's one group we've left out so far. Can anyone think of who that might be? (*Pause for answers.*) The magi, that's right.

We've saved the magi until today, because the church gives them their own special day. That day is January sixth and is called 'Epiphany,' Today is Epiphany Sunday. Today we're going to learn about the magi. (*Set up the flannel board with small stars dotting the sky.*)

Jesus was born in Bethlehem. The Bible tells us that soon after Jesus was born, some men who studied the stars came from the East looking for him. People who study the stars are called astrologers. These astrologers studied the stars every night. (*Put magi on right side of the board.*) One night, they noticed something different in the sky—a new star. (*Put Bethlehem star on far left side of board.*) The astrologers believed that a new star in the sky meant something important. They believed it meant a new king had been born. So they decided to follow the new star. (*Put camels with magi.*)

The star led them far from their home in the East to the small country of Judah. (*Put Jerusalem in center of flannel board.*) They went to the capital city of Jerusalem and asked the people there where the baby born to be ruler of the Jews was. "We saw the new star set in the sky to celebrate his birth. We have come to worship him," the magi said.

When King Herod heard about this, he was very upset. He didn't know anything about a new star or a baby who would one day take his place as king, and he didn't like the idea, either. He called together all of *his* wise counselors, the chief priests and teachers of the law. He asked them where the scriptures said the Messiah would be born. They told him Bethlehem.

So Herod invited the astrologers to a secret meeting. *(Place Herod with astrologers in Jerusalem on flannel board.)* He told them to look in Bethlehem for the baby. "And when you find him, tell me where he is, so that I may go and worship him, too," he said.

They left Jerusalem and headed toward Bethlehem. On the way, they saw the star again, and it led them to the place where Jesus was. They went inside and saw the child with his mother, Mary.

I wonder what Mary thought when the astrologers came into the stable. The men were rich, and wore beautiful, fine clothes. They didn't look like they were from Judah, either. They were covered with dust from their long journey. Mary may have wondered what these people from so far away were doing there. They gave her an answer right away. They knelt down and worshiped Jesus. *(Put kneeling astrologers in place.)*

These astrologers were truly wise people. Being wise is not the same thing as being smart. Being smart is knowing lots of stuff—like two plus two equals four, or that Laura Ingalls Wilder wrote *Little House on the Prairie*. Being wise is understanding things. The Eastern astrologers understood that Jesus was special. They knew that he had come from God and understood that he deserved their worship and respect. They gave him gifts—gold frankincense, and myrrh.

When it came time for the magi to go home, they went a different way. God warned them in a dream not to tell Herod where Jesus was. Herod didn't really want to worship Jesus; he wanted to hurt him. Herod wasn't wise at all. He was smart enough to know that Jesus was sent from God, that he was the Messiah. But Herod did not understand what that meant.

Let's Pray. Dear God, make us truly wise. Help us to know the stories in the Bible and to understand their teachings. Amen.

On Being Baptized

Prop Needed
Your church's baptismal font with water in it

The Message
This morning I want to begin our time together by showing you something I'm sure you've seen before. You see it here in the sanctuary every Sunday when you come to church. We only use it once in a while, though. Can you guess what it is? (*Allow children to respond.*) Here's another clue. It has water in it. Now can you guess? (*Pause for answer.*) That's right. It's the thing we use for baptism. It's called a baptismal font.

Have any of you seen a baptism here at church? Do you remember what happened? (*Pause for answers.*) The minister asks the people being baptized whether or not they love Jesus and want to follow Jesus' teachings. If a baby or small child is being baptized, the minister asks the parents. Who is our minister? (*Pause.*) Pastor Denise. So, after the person or parents answer 'Yes,' Pastor Denise dips her hand in the water. She puts her wet hand on the person's head and says, "I baptize you in the name of the Father, and of the Son, and of the Holy Spirit."

Do any of you remember your own baptism? I was baptized when I was a baby, so I don't remember it. (*If this situation doesn't apply to you, briefly recount your own baptism.*) If you don't remember your baptism, ask your mom or dad if you've been baptized when you get home. If you have, ask them what they remember about it.

Jesus was baptized when he was thirty years old. His cousin, John, was preaching and baptizing people at the Jordan River, and Jesus went to the river to be baptized by him.

John was a very interesting character. In fact, many people probably thought he was a kook. He wore clothes made out of camel's hair, with a leather belt around his waist. For food he ate locusts, which are kind of like grasshoppers, and wild honey. He told the people that they had to change their lives. They needed to stop sinning and turn to God. They needed to get ready for God's chosen one, the Messiah, to come.

When John saw Jesus coming to be baptized, he was very surprised. This was God's chosen one, the special person God had sent into the world to teach people about God's love. John did not think he was good enough to baptize Jesus. He said, "I should not baptize you. You should baptize me instead." But Jesus told John that God wanted him to be baptized, so John agreed to do it.

John and Jesus walked into the Jordan River. When John baptized people, they got really wet! There, in the Jordan River, John baptized Jesus. The Bible tells us that when Jesus came out of the water, heaven opened up. The spirit of God came down like a dove and rested on him. Then God's voice said from heaven, "This is my own dear son, with whom I am pleased."

At that moment, both John and Jesus knew that they had done the right thing. God was happy that Jesus was baptized.

For three years after his baptism, Jesus went on to teach and preach and heal people. He had twelve close friends, called disciples, who helped him with his work. One of the last things Jesus told his disciples was to go out into the world and preach the good news about Jesus and God's love. When people believed what the disciples told them and wanted to become Christians, Jesus told the disciples to baptize them, just as Jesus had been baptized. Even today, people who love Jesus are baptized. People who want their children to grow up knowing Jesus as their friend have their babies baptized as well. Being baptized means we're part of a loving family, the family of God.

Let's Pray. Dear God, thank you for sending your child Jesus into the world to show us your love and how you want us to live. In Jesus' name. Amen.

(You may want to invite the children up to the font for a closer look as they leave.)

Jesus Is the Light

Props Needed
Candle
Matches
Guitar or piano accompaniment
Song leader (yourself, or someone from the congregation)

The Message
Have any of you ever been in a power failure? A power failure is when the electricity doesn't work. Maybe you're watching TV in the evening and all of a sudden . . . it's like someone pulled all the plugs at once! (*Turn off the sanctuary lights.*) The TV shuts off. All the lights go out. You find yourself sitting in the dark. A power failure can be kind of scary, can't it? Usually the grown-ups in the family will stumble around in the dark until some candles and matches can be found. Then they will light a candle so it isn't so dark anymore (*light candle*).

Before Jesus was born, it was as if the whole world was involved in one gigantic power failure. It was as if everyone were stumbling around in the dark, trying to find God. Jesus came to show each of us the way to God. That is why he is called the 'light of the world.' Jesus acts like a candle in the darkness, lighting the way to God.

There's a song about Jesus being the light of the world, and we're going to learn it this morning. It's called "Jesus Is the Light." Mrs. Johnson is going to teach it to us. (*Teach the children the song, phrase by phrase. Encourage the congregation to sing along. Have fun!*)

Let's Pray. Dear God, thank you for sending Jesus to light the way so that we might find you. Amen.

Jesus Is the Light of the World

Tune by W. W. Umla

Je - sus is the light of the world, Je - sus is the

light of the world, Je - sus is the light of the world

and he's ev - er - shin - ing in my soul.

He's the light of the world, he's the light of the world,

he's the light, he's the light of the world.

23

Jesus Calls Us

Props Needed

A friendship bracelet (these are bracelets woven of colored thread, handmade or sold where children's party favors are found)

One friendship bracelet for each child

The Message

Today I have with me a special piece of jewelry. It isn't expensive, and it didn't come from a fancy jewelry store, but it's very special anyway. (*Show the bracelet.*) It's called a friendship bracelet. What makes this bracelet so special is that one friend gives it to another. Then, when the person who was given the bracelet looks at it, he or she thinks of the friend who gave it and how much the friendship they share means.

Jesus had twelve friends who were very important to him. Those twelve friends were called his disciples. The disciples were ordinary people Jesus asked to follow him. The first four people Jesus found to be his disciples were fishermen.

One day Jesus was walking along the shore of Lake Galilee. There he saw two fishermen catching fish in a big, round net. The fishermen were brothers. Their names were Simon and Andrew. Jesus said to them, "Come with me, and I will teach you to catch men and women for God." Simon and Andrew left their nets behind and followed Jesus.

Jesus went further down the beach and saw two other brothers. Their names were James and John. They and their father, Zebedee, were fishing from a boat. Jesus called them too. "Come with me," he said. James and John left their boat and followed Jesus.

Simon, Andrew, James, and John were the first people Jesus chose to be his disciples. No one knows why they left their fishing businesses behind to follow him. Maybe they had heard about Jesus and the good works he did—teaching people about God, healing the sick, and helping the poor. Or maybe they knew when they saw Jesus that there was something special about him, and they wanted to find out what it was. The important thing is not why they followed, but that they did follow Jesus.

The twelve disciples were very important to Jesus and to the world. Jesus taught them as much as they could learn about God and what it meant to be in the family of God. They learned, not only from what Jesus said, but also from how Jesus lived his life. They watched how Jesus loved God and other people and tried to be more like him. The disciples were Jesus' friends, his students, and his helpers. They helped Jesus with his work—or ministry— of teaching, preaching, and healing. And they kept on doing Jesus' work even after he had been crucified. If the disciples hadn't spread the news of Jesus and the lessons he taught, we might not know about Jesus today.

The Bible lists twelve disciples by name. But Jesus never stopped asking people to follow him. For almost two thousand years, people from every part of the world have chosen to be Jesus' disciples—to learn from him, to help him with his work, and to be his friends. Today we call these people 'the church.' We in the church are Jesus' modern-day disciples.

I have a gift for each one of you this morning. (*Begin tying friendship bracelets on the children's wrists.*) When you look at this friendship bracelet, remember that you are Jesus' disciple. You are Jesus' very special friend. Having you for a friend makes Jesus very happy.

Let's Pray. Dear God, thank you for sending us a wonderful friend like Jesus. Help us to learn from his teachings and to carry on his work by helping others. In our friend Jesus' name. Amen.

Breaking Walls Building Peace

Prop Needed
A set of large children's building blocks

The Message
Good morning, everyone. How many of you like to build things with blocks? (*Bring out blocks.*) What do you like to build with blocks? (*Listen to answers.*) Do any of you ever like to build walls? It's fun to see how wide and how high you can make a wall before it falls down, isn't it?

Walls can be good things. They hold up the roofs of houses and other buildings. They keep the cold rain out and the warm air in. If you go inside your room at home and close the door, you can have a quiet place to take a nap, read a book, or be alone to think. Your room wouldn't be so nice and quiet without walls, would it? Without walls, you wouldn't have a room at all!

Outside walls can be helpful too. They can tell us where our yard stops and the neighbor's yard starts. They can keep the dog in so it won't run into the street and get hurt by a car. All these are good reasons to build walls.

But walls can also be bad. Thousands of years ago, there was a country that had many enemies. That country built a huge wall to keep its enemies out. Guards were posted on top of the wall and told to kill anyone from the outside who came near it. The wall was so strong that it still stands today. It is called the Great Wall of China. It's sad to think that countries cannot get along with one another and that walls need to be built between them.

Walls made of brick or stone are not the only kind that people build between themselves. Sometimes we put up invisible walls to shut other people out. We do and say things that separate us from one another, things that make us not as close to one another as God wants us to be.

If I call a person a mean name, that's like putting a block in the wall between myself and that other person. (*Begin building a wall with the blocks, adding one or two blocks with each example you give, until you have a fairly good-sized wall.*) I hurt the other person's feelings with that mean name, and at least for a little while we aren't as good of friends as we were before I called the name. If I cheat on a game with a friend, that's like adding a block to the wall between us. If I promise to play with one friend and then go play with someone else, there's another brick in the wall.

Any time we lie, break a promise, or hurt another person's feelings (*add three blocks*), we add more bricks to the wall. If we hurt a person by hitting or kicking or shoving, the wall gets higher and higher. If we refuse to share or grab a toy or copy papers at school, we're adding more and more bricks.

God doesn't like to see people divided by walls, whether they're real walls like the Great Wall of China or invisible walls built with hurt feelings. God wants us all to love and care for each other. One reason God sent Jesus was to break down the walls that divide us. Jesus is sometimes called the 'Prince of Peace.' Jesus teaches us to treat each other with love and fairness. When we make mistakes and hurt each other's feelings, Jesus teaches us to forgive each other. Jesus teaches us to be peacemakers.

Will all of you be peacemakers for Jesus and knock down this ugly wall I've built?

Let's Pray. Dear God, help us to be peacemakers, to treat other people with fairness and love, and to forgive those who've hurt us. In the name of Jesus, the 'Prince of Peace.' Amen.

Lighting the World with Love

Props Needed

Several candles in candleholders or votives on a tray
One candle that is a different color than the rest

The Message

How many names do you think I have? Anybody want to guess (*Pause for answers.*) What are my names? (*Pause again.*) That's good. Two of my names are Dianne and Deming. My middle name is Elise. My maiden name—the name I had before I was married—is Jones. But I go by other names too. Some people call me 'Reverend' or 'Pastor.' Two people call me 'Mom' or 'Mommy.' My husband calls me 'Honey,' and some people call me 'Mrs. Deming.' If you think about it, you probably have lots of names and nicknames too.

Jesus had many names. He was called 'Prince of Peace,' 'Son of God,' 'Christ,' 'Messiah,' 'Teacher,' 'Rabbi,' and 'Light of the World.' (*Light the different-colored candle.*) The Bible calls Jesus the light of the world.

Once, when Jesus was talking to his followers, he called *them* the light of the world. How could that be? If Jesus is the light, how can others, even those who follow him, also be the light?

Have you ever noticed something funny about light? Light can be passed from one candle to another, and both candles stay lit. (*Use one candle to light another. As you talk, slowly light the other candles from the first one until all are lit.*) The first candle doesn't go out or lose its light just because it passes light onto another candle. In fact, each time the candle is used to light another, more light shines instead of less.

The same thing is true with the light of God's love. Jesus passed the light of God's love on to his disciples and other followers. Today, Jesus still shares the light of God's love with those who love him. Jesus passes the light to us. We are the light of the world now.

How might we let the light of God's love shine in our lives? We can be kind to others. We can be helpful to our parents and teachers. We can share our toys with our brothers or sisters, and play cooperatively with our friends. We can give some of what we have to the poor by bringing food to the food bank. We can live our lives caring about other people and not just ourselves. In these ways, we light up the world with God's love. You help to make this world a brighter, happier place.

Let's Pray. Dear God, may our lives glow with the warm rays of your love, so that our corner of the world might be a brighter, happier place. In Jesus' name. Amen.

The Right Tool for the Job

Props Needed

Several kitchen tools, such as a spoon, bowl, mixer, pans, sifter, grater, and can opener

The Message

Do any of you know how to cook? What kinds of things do you like to cook? (*Listen to answers.*) Some people's job is to cook for other people—at a restaurant, in a school cafeteria, or for the army. These cooks are sometimes called chefs.

Anybody who wants to cook needs certain tools. Your kitchen is probably full of cooking tools. I've brought some cooking tools with me today. Help me figure out what each thing is.

Who knows what this tool is? (*Hold up spoon.*) A spoon, of course! A cook uses a spoon to mix up ingredients in one of these (*hold up bowl*), a bowl. How about this tool? What is this? (*Hold up sifter.*) Yes, a sifter. A sifter works the lumps out of dry ingredients such as flour and fluffs them up. Tell me what the rest of these cooking tools are. (*Hold them up one at a time and allow children to identify.*) A cook needs kitchen tools in order to get his or her job done. Without the proper tools, cooks or chefs could not do their work.

People in other jobs needs tools to get their jobs done, too. What tools does a fire fighter need to put out a fire? (*Pause for answers.*) Yes, a fire fighter needs a ladder, an ax, a hose, and a hook. What about a barber or a hairdresser? What tools does someone who cuts hair for a living need? (*Pause.*) Scissors, combs, brushes—good. What tools does a doctor need? (*Listen to children's answers.*) Very good.

Lots of jobs need tools. A person in business needs a computer. A teacher needs pens and pencils, books, chalkboards, and many other tools. A gardener needs a rake, a hoe, a lawn mower, and a trowel. It takes tools to do almost any job I can think of.

As Christians, you and I have a very important job to do. Our job is to share the story of Jesus and God's love and to live our lives in a way that makes the world a better place. That is a big job, isn't it? God understands what a hard job it is to be a Christian and has given us a tool we need to get the job done. That tool is the Bible.

The Bible tells us what we need to know to do our job as Christians. In stories, poems, and letters, the Bible explains what is expected of the people of God, and how others before us have done a good job or a bad job. We can learn from what happened to them and be better people of God ourselves. The Bible also teaches us about God's love. God loves us so much that even when we make mistakes and disappoint our parents, our friends, ourselves, and God, the Lord forgives us.

To do a good job, a Christian needs the Bible just as much as a chef needs a spoon and bowl. And just as a spoon and bowl aren't any help if they sit unused in a drawer, the Bible is no help if it sits unopened on a shelf. We have to read the Bible for it to be helpful to us. So the next time you're ready for a good story, ask your mom or dad to read or tell you one from the Bible. God has given us a great tool. Let's not forget to use it.

Let's Pray. Dear God, thank you for giving us the tools we need to build a Christian life. As we read the Bible, help us to understand your teachings and to grow in faith and practice. Amen.

Amigo the Dog

Prop Needed
None

The Message
Good morning, boys and girls. Who can tell me what a missionary is? (*Listen to answers.*) A missionary is someone who works for God and the church among the poor. There are many different kinds of missionaries. Some missionaries are doctors. They heal people in clinics and hospitals in poor or out-of-the-way areas where there aren't any ordinary doctors. Some missionaries are farmers. They help farmers in poor areas grow better crops. Engineers, teachers, and ministers are some other types of missionaries. Missionaries often work in other countries. Our story this morning is about a missionary sent by the church to be a pastor in Africa.

This missionary was sent to a small African village, where he and his wife lived in a hut just as the local villagers did. They brought a few things with them from the United States, but their new home still seemed strange and lonely.

They were only in the village a few days when the missionary found out that he needed to go to a church meeting a hundred miles away. The meeting was three days long, and he would need to spend two nights away. He was not allowed to take his wife with him, and he didn't like the idea of leaving her in the village alone, because they hadn't made any friends yet. He didn't know if anyone would help her—a stranger—if she should have a problem and need someone. But she told him, "You go on to your meeting. I can take care of myself. And besides, I am not alone. The Lord is always with me."

So the missionary left the next morning for the meeting. His wife spent the day unpacking the last of their things. At four-thirty, just before it started to get dark, she took a can of trash outside and was greeted by a large black dog. The dog followed her to the burn barrel at back of the hut and then back up onto the porch. When the woman went inside the hut, the dog stood at the door and waited. She turned around and looked at him. He cocked his head. "Do you want to come in and keep me company?" she asked. And when she opened the door the dog walked right in.

She fixed her supper and gave some to the dog. "What is your name?" she asked. "My name is Alice. I think I'll call you Amigo. That means 'friend' in Spanish."

After supper, Alice washed the dishes, then read a book. Finally, she gave Amigo a pat on the head and went to bed. The first thing the next morning, she opened the door for the dog to go out. She was sorry to see him run down the village street and into the brush. She would miss her only friend in the village.

Alice spent the day making plans for the Sunday school classes she would be helping to teach in the village church. At about four-thirty, she got up from her writing table, stretched her arms up toward the ceiling, and decided to go for a walk before supper. When she stepped outside, who should she see coming toward her but her friend Amigo. They took a walk together and then went inside to eat. After supper, Amigo fell asleep by the stove.

In the middle of the night, Alice woke up because she heard Amigo barking loudly and the sound of something being knocked over. She switched on the light just in time to see two burglars running out the front door. "Good boy, Amigo," she said. "You protected me from those robbers."

The next morning when Alice let Amigo out, he took off again. "See you tonight, Amigo!" she called. That afternoon when the missionary came home, Alice told him about her new friend and the robbers he had scared away. "It's four-thirty now," she said. "Amigo should be here any second now." They waited, but the big black dog didn't show up. Alice never saw Amigo again.

You may wonder sometimes how God can take care of everyone at once. God takes care of us in many different ways. God gives us minds so we can figure out a lot of problems on our own. God gives us people to care for us—parents, grandparents, teachers, neighbors, ministers, doctors, and friends. God hopes that with God's help we will all take care of each other. And other times God works in truly mysterious ways—like having a big black dog wander by just when we need him. It is important for us to remember that we can trust and depend upon God to help us, to love us, and to be our friend always.

Let's Pray. Our dear friend God, thank you for always being there for us. May we be there for others and in that way help you care for your children. Amen.

Choosing Sides

Props Needed
Two toy soldiers from opposing armies

The Message
Good morning, girls and boys. Today I have two toys to show you. (*Hold up toys.*) They are toy soldiers. One has on a red uniform, and the other a blue uniform. (*Adapt description to your particular examples.*) Why do you think these soldiers are wearing different colored uniforms? (*Pause for answers.*) Because they are from different armies.

If you were playing a game of war with soldiers like these, you might line up all the red soldiers on one side of the play area, and all the blue soldiers on the other side. Then you and your friends could take turns pretending the soldiers are shooting and killing each other until the side with the most soldiers left wins. Soldiers on opposite sides in a war are called 'enemies,' aren't they?

Playing war can be fun, but real war is not a game, and being in a real war is no fun at all. Real soldiers are human beings like you and me. If a real soldier gets shot, he bleeds. If a real soldier dies, she's dead. You can't just stand everybody up and start the game all over again like you can with toy soldiers. Real war is so terrible that many parents don't like their children to play war games.

Our story this morning is about a real soldier in a real war and his father.* The war was World War Two. It took place about forty-five years ago, in the nineteen forties. Our country was at war with Japan. The United States and Japan were enemies.

A young soldier was going off to war to fight the Japanese. His father held him tight before putting him on the train and waving good-bye. The father was sad to see his son go, and worried that

---

*This story is based on one that appeared in *The Pastor's Story File* newsletter, January 1986.

he might never see him again. He was so worried that, as the train rolled down the track, he thought to himself, "If my son is killed, I hope every Japanese soldier is killed, too." But even as he thought these words, they did not sound right to him. He knew that it was wrong to hate, no matter what happened to his son. And at that moment he made a choice. "I will not hate," he said. "I choose not to be destroyed by hate."

A year later, the father received the news he had hoped he would never hear. His son had been killed in the war. Soon after, his son's life insurance money arrived. It was ten thousand dollars. Again, the father made a choice. He chose to send the ten thousand dollars to his church's mission board and asked that it be used to buy food and medicine for the Japanese.

Jesus taught us to love our enemies. I hope none of you ever has to fight in or lose someone you love in a war. All of us have people we don't get along with very well, and we can choose to love rather than hate them. We can choose to treat them with kindness and respect. Once we've made that decision, we might find that we've made a new friend out of an old enemy.

Let's Pray. Dear God, if only all people and all governments could learn to get along with each other, there would be no war. Help us to learn and live your lessons. In Jesus' name. Amen.

A Gift to See

Props and Preparation Needed
Flannel board
Flannel-board figures (found in the Appendix)
Make a 'transfigured' Jesus by coating figure with a thin film of white glue then with white or silver glitter. Make the shining cloud in the same way

The Message
Does anyone know what makes this coming Wednesday special? (*Pause.*) It is what we call Ash Wednesday. Ash Wednesday begins the season of the church year called Lent. During Lent, we remember the things that happened to Jesus right before he died. Many of these things were bad. People plotted against him behind his back. He was arrested, lied about, and beaten. But before any of these bad things took place, something very wonderful happened. I want to tell you that story today.

(*Set up flannel board with mountain in center. Follow story with figures.*)

One day Jesus took Peter, James, and John with him on a walk. Remember that these three were the first disciples Jesus chose. They had all done the same thing for a living. Do you remember what their jobs were before they were disciples? (*Pause for answers.*) They were fishermen, that's right.

Jesus led his three friends up a high mountain where they were all alone. Then an amazing thing happened. Jesus started to change, right before his disciples' eyes. His face was shining like the sun, and his clothes were dazzling white. (*Overlay plain Jesus figure with 'transfigured' Jesus.*) Then the three disciples saw Moses and Elijah, two men of God from Israel's history, talking with Jesus.

Peter was so excited, he said to Jesus, "Lord, it is so good that we are here. We could build three places of worship here—one for you, one for Moses, and one for Elijah!"

Just then a shining cloud came over them. A voice from the cloud said, "This is my own dear son. I am very proud of him. Now be quiet and listen to him."

When Peter, James, and John heard the voice, they were terrified. They fell face-down on the ground. But then Jesus came over to them and touched them. "Don't be afraid," he said. When they looked up, Jesus was the only other person there, and he looked like his old self again.

As they walked down the mountain, Jesus said to his friends, "Don't tell anyone about the vision you just saw until I have been raised from the dead."

Jesus gave his friends a gift that day. They didn't understand it at the time, but they would remember the gift of the vision later. After the pain, after the arrest, after the trial, after the embarrassment and humiliation, after Jesus' death, they remembered the gift of their vision. They remembered Jesus standing with Moses and Elijah. They remembered his shining face and his dazzling clothes, and they knew that everything was all right. Jesus was alive and well with God. And they knew that someday they would see their friend Jesus again—in heaven.

Let's Pray. Dear God, thank you for visions and dreams and your promise of eternal life. In our savior's name we pray. Amen.

Season of Lent

Thy
Will   Be
Done

Lead Me Not into Temptation

Prop Needed
A chocolate chip cookie

The Message
Today we're going to talk about temptation. That's a big word, *temptation*. Can you all say it with me? Temptation. Good! Does anyone know what temptation means? (*Pause for answers.*) Temptation is when a part of you wants to do something or say something that the rest of you knows is really wrong. Let me give you some examples.

Imagine that your dad has spent the afternoon baking cookies. The delicious smell of melted chocolate chips fills the whole house. You were allowed two of the cookies at three-thirty. Now it's five o'clock, just an hour before dinner. You ask if you may please have just one more cookie. You are told, "No, you'll spoil your dinner." A few minutes later, you are all alone in the kitchen. The countertops are covered with cookies like this one (*hold up cookie*), cooling on racks. No one would notice just one cookie missing. You are *tempted* to take one and eat it, even though you know you're not supposed to. Wanting to take the cookie when you know you're not allowed is called 'temptation.'

Another kind of temptation might be cheating at school. What if you didn't do your math homework one night? Your favorite show was on TV, and you watched it instead of doing your homework. On the bus the next day, you remember that you didn't get your math done. You tell your problem to your best friend, who is sitting next to you and who offers to let you copy. You are *tempted* to copy and hand it in so you won't get a zero for the day. After all, it's just one night's homework—no big deal. Wanting to copy your friend's homework when you know it's wrong is called 'temptation.'

Imagine that you're playing blocks with a friend. Together, you are building a skyscraper. Your friend decides that she wants to be the one to knock down the building, so she kicks it before it's finished. This makes you really mad. You're so angry, you are *tempted* to punch her or call her a mean name, but you know you shouldn't. Wanting to hurt another person, even if they are wrong, is called 'temptation.'

There are many different kinds of temptation. If you have ever been tempted to do something you know is wrong, raise your hand. Everyone is tempted sometimes. Even Jesus was tempted. There's nothing wrong with being tempted. What you choose to *do* when you are tempted can be either right or wrong.

If you were tempted to eat cookies when you were told not to, what would you do? (*Listen to answers.*) If you hadn't done your homework and your friend offered to let you copy his, what would you do? (*Listen.*) And when you feel like hurting someone else by punching her or calling her names, what would you do? (*Listen.*)

We don't always do the right thing, do we? Sometimes we give in to temptation when we should say, "No, that is wrong." Sometimes we try to blame someone else when we give in to temptation. We might say, "Well, he offered to let me copy his homework," or "She knocked down the building first." But the truth is, when you give in to temptation and do something wrong, it is your choice. The only person you can blame is yourself. Part of growing up is learning to say "no" to things we know are wrong, even if we want them very, very badly.

The choices are not always easy. Sometimes it is hard to know what is the right thing and what is the wrong thing to do. Sometimes it helps to talk about the choices you have to make with a grown-up you trust. Talking to God in prayer can be helpful, too. God wants to help us make the right choices in life, because God loves us always.

Let's Pray. Dear God, when we are faced with temptation, please help us to say "no." Help us to do the right thing, and forgive us when we fail. In Jesus' name. Amen.

God's Amazing Grace

Prop Needed
A hymnal opened to "Amazing Grace"

The Message
Can anyone tell me what a Christian is? (*Listen to answers.*)
Christians are people who know that God loves them and forgives
them when they make mistakes. They believe that God sent
Jesus into the world to show us God's amazing love for us, and to
be our friend and savior. Christians come to church to worship
God, to give thanks for God's goodness to us, to learn about God
and Jesus, and to serve the Lord by helping others.

People become Christians in many different ways. Each person
in this sanctuary has his or her own story about how he or she
grew to understand God's love and to love God in return.

Many people here were blessed to grow up knowing about God's
love. Their parents were Christians who brought them to church
each Sunday. They learned about God and Jesus in Sunday
school and at home. They have known Jesus as their friend for as
long as they can remember. In this way, they are like most of you.
Knowing God's love and growing in faith through your whole life
is a very special blessing.

Other people don't become Christians until they are older. One
person who didn't believe until he was a grown-up was a man
named John Newton.*

John Newton lived more than two hundred and fifty years ago.
He was born in 1725, and his mother died when he was only seven
years old. His father was a sea captain, and when John was eleven
he left school and went to work on his father's ship. He worked
on several ships and finally, when he was older, became the captain of his own ship. It sounds like John Newton was doing very
well, doesn't it? But there was just one problem. His ship was a
slave ship.

*Story of John Newton from *101 Hymn Stories* by Kenneth W. Osbeck. ©
1982 by Kregel Publications, a division of Kregel, Inc., P.O. Box 2607, Grand
Rapids, MI 49501. Used by permission.

Back in those days, people from Europe and North America went to Africa to capture slaves. They kidnapped the native Africans and put them on slave ships. These ships traveled to the West Indies and North American, where the slaves were sold and forced to work on big farms called plantations. On the ships, the Africans were treated cruelly. They were not given enough food and water. They got sick from living all crowded together in the dirty hulls of the ships, and many of them died before they reached land. This was the kind of ship John Newton captained.

On March 10, 1748, Mr. Newton and his crew were returning to England from Africa when their ship was caught in a terrible storm. They all thought the ship would sink and they would drown. Mr. Newton began reading a book called *Imitation of Christ* written by a Christian monk. The frightening storm plus the message of God's love and forgiveness in Jesus that John Newton found in the book caused him to believe in God and ask Jesus to be his friend. John Newton, slave trader, became a Christian.

For a while, he stayed captain of his ship and tried to make life better for the slaves aboard. But soon he realized that taking away the freedom of other human beings and selling them as slaves was wrong, and for the rest of his life he worked to make slavery illegal in his home country of England.

Mr. Newton got married and worked as a clerk for nine years until he finally became a minister. John Newton also wrote some hymns, one of which tells how he felt about becoming a Christian. It's called "Amazing Grace." (*Show children the hymn in your hymnbook.*) We still sing "Amazing Grace" today. *Grace* is another word for God's love and forgiveness for us. It's the thing that we Christians believe in and cherish most. The words to Mr. Newton's song go like this . . . (*Read the words to the first verse.*)

It does not matter how a person comes to learn of God's grace. Whether one grows up as a Christian or becomes a Christian later in life is not important. What *is* important is that we know that God loves the world so much that God sent Jesus, and that whoever believes in Jesus should not perish but have everlasting life.

Let's Pray. Dear God, we thank you for your love and forgiveness. Thank you for sending your child Jesus, the Christ, to show us that amazing grace. Amen.

(*As the children return to their seats, you may want to have a soloist, the choir, or the congregation sing "Amazing Grace."*)

What's on the Inside?

Props Needed
A sampler box of chocolates (if the fillings are described on the lid, cover the descriptions so the children can't see them)

A napkin for each child

A few pastel bonbons or other non-chocolate treats for those who may be allergic to chocolate

The Message
I have a special treat for you this morning. First I want to give each of you a napkin. (*Pass out napkins.*) How many of you like chocolate? (*Bring out chocolates and open the box.*) I'd like each of you to take one piece of candy, but don't eat it yet. Place it on your napkin until I tell you that you may eat it. (*Pass around the box, and let each child choose a piece. While the box is being passed, ask if anyone is unable to eat chocolate. If so, give those children alternative treats.*) Okay, does everyone have a piece? Good.

You each chose a piece of candy. These candies have chocolate on the outside and some kind of filling on the inside. Some have vanilla cream and some have butter cream, strawberry, fudge, nougat, caramel, cherry, or coconut. Can you tell by looking at the outside what is on the inside of your piece of candy? (*Pause for answers.*) You really can't tell, can you? Go ahead now and take a bite. Look at what's inside your chocolate. What kind did you get? (*Pause for answers.*)

People are a lot like those chocolates. We can't tell who a person is just by looking at the outside. Whether people are men or women, old or young, large or small—no matter what color their skin is or what country they're from—these outside things don't really tell us who people are. We need to get to know what a person thinks and feels, what she likes and doesn't like, what makes her happy or sad, what she enjoys doing, and what she believes.

You have to get to know a person on the inside to know what she's like and who she is.*

Jesus knew how important it was to get to know people on the inside before deciding what they were like. In his day, there were many rules. Men weren't supposed to talk to women they didn't know. Jews weren't supposed to share dishes with Samaritans. Decent people weren't supposed to have anything to do with people they thought didn't live a good life.

One day Jesus, who was a Jew, was traveling in Samaria, when he met a woman at the town well. He was thirsty, so Jesus, a Jewish man, asked the Samaritan woman for a drink of water from her cup. He broke all the rules. Jesus knew that to decide the woman wasn't worth knowing because of what she was on the outside wasn't fair. Jesus talked to the Samaritan woman for a long time. By the end of their conversation, the woman believed that Jesus was God's chosen one, sent to save the world. She ran through the streets of the town, telling everyone about the special person, Jesus. Because of her faith, many people in that town believed and became Christians.

If Jesus had only looked at that person on the outside—as a Samaritan and a woman with a bad reputation—and failed to get to know her on the inside, the people of that town would have never learned the good news of Jesus and God's love. They would have missed out. The woman would have missed out. And Jesus would have missed out, too. You can't tell what the filling is by looking only at the outside of a chocolate candy, and you can't tell who a person is by looking only at the outside.

Let's Pray. Dear God, we are sometimes quick to decide what a person is like without taking the time to really find out. Forgive us, Lord, and help us to love our neighbors as we love ourselves. Amen.

*Based on a children's sermon delivered by the Reverend Lucinda Stafford-Lewis.

FOURTH SUNDAY OF LENT   Spiritual Blindness
John 9:1–41

On Healing Blindness

Prop Needed
One blindfold for each child

The Message
Who can tell me what we mean when we say that someone is blind? (*Pause for answers.*) That's right. Being blind means not being able to see. Have you ever wondered what it would be like to be blind? Not being able to see would make many things hard to do, wouldn't it?

Let's do an experiment. Everyone stand up and get in a line. I have a blindfold for each one of you. (*Tie blindfolds on the children.*) Now hold hands with the person on either side of you. We're going to take a little walk. (*Slowly lead the children around the sanctuary. If some are too frightened to try the exercise, tell them to wait for you at the storytelling place. When everyone returns to the point of origin, resume the message.*)

Okay now, keep your blindfold on a moment. Go ahead and sit down. How does it feel to be blind? (*Listen to answers.*) Being blind makes even a simple thing like walking around a room difficult, doesn't it? You may take the blindfold off your head now. Imagine if you couldn't just take a blindfold off to see again, but were blind all the time—how hard that would be.

Being physically blind is when you can't see the world around you, and it is hard. But did you know there is another kind of blindness, too? That is being spiritually blind. Being spiritually blind means not understanding or believing in God. It is even harder to go through life being spiritually blind than it is to be physically blind.

Jesus said that he came into our world to give sight to the blind. He healed some people of their physical blindness so that they were able to see the world around them. He also healed some people of their spiritual blindness and helped them to see, or understand, God. We can't see God like we see the person sit-

46

ting next to us, but Jesus helps us to know and understand God. Jesus helps us to feel God's love and to see that love at work in our world. Jesus still heals our blindness and helps us to see and understand God today.

Let's Pray. Dear God, even though we cannot see you in the physical sense as we can see the people sitting next to us, we want to see you in the spiritual sense—to know and understand you and to see your power at work in our lives and the world. May we be given this blessing. Amen.

John 11:1–45

Three from Bethany

Props Needed
Flannel board
Flannel-board figures (found in the Appendix)

The Message
We talk a lot about Jesus' friends, the twelve disciples. Jesus had many other friends, too. Three people who were very special to him were Martha, Mary, and Lazarus. They were sisters and brother and lived together in the same house in a town called Bethany. One day, Jesus received a message from Martha and Mary that said, "Your dear friend Lazarus is sick." (*Follow the story with flannel-board figures. Start with Jesus and his disciples receiving the message.*)

Jesus loved his friends from Bethany, but when he got the news he stayed where he was for two more days instead of rushing immediately away. Finally, he said to his disciples, "Let's go back to Judea and help Lazarus."

The disciples were upset. The last time Jesus had visited that area, some people tried to kill him. The disciples knew it was not safe for him to go there. But Jesus knew he had to go. He needed to save his friend, and he needed to show everyone the power of God at work.

So Jesus and his disciples traveled to Bethany. They reached the edge of town and learned that Lazarus was dead. (*Put outline of town on flannel board and the cave in one corner.*)

Martha heard that Jesus was on his way and ran to the edge of town to meet him. When she saw Jesus, she said, "Lord, if you had been here, my brother would not have died. But even now I know that God will give you whatever you ask. . . . "

"Your brother will rise again," Jesus told her.

"I know," she replied, "that he will rise again in the resurrection on the last day."

Jesus said to her, "I am the resurrection and the life. Those who believe in me, even though they die, will live, and everyone who lives and believes in me will never die. Do you believe this?" "Yes, Lord!" Martha answered. "I believe you are the Messiah, God's chosen one sent to save the world from death."

Martha went back to her house to get her sister, Mary. She too met Jesus and said to him, "If you had been here, my brother would not have died." By now, Martha, Mary, and all their friends were standing at the edge of town with Jesus. Everyone was very sad about Lazarus's death and was crying. Jesus cried with them. He led the group up to the tomb where Lazarus was buried.

The tomb was a cave with a large stone covering the opening, and Jesus told the people to take the stone away. Martha was a very practical person, however. She knew that a body that had been buried for four days would start to smell—badly. She reminded Jesus of this and told him that it might not be such a good idea to take away the stone. "It will stink," she said, "because he has been buried four days!"

Then Jesus reminded her, "Didn't I tell you that you would see God's power at work if you believed?"

The stone was taken away from the opening of the tomb, and Jesus said a prayer. Then he said in a loud voice, "Lazarus, come out!" Lazarus walked out of the tomb. His body was wrapped in grave cloths, and he had a cloth covering his face. "Untie the cloths," Jesus told them, "and let him go."

Martha and Mary were very happy that Lazarus had been brought back to life. Many of the visiting friends had seen what Jesus did, and they believed in him. But other people did not like what Jesus did. They did not like the power Jesus had. They thought too many people were beginning to believe in him and listen to him. They were afraid that people would stop listening to the religious leaders in Jerusalem. So the people who didn't like Jesus went to Jerusalem and told the religious leaders about what had happened in Bethany. The leaders were not pleased and began to plot against Jesus.

Let's Pray. Dear God, thank you for the power of your love. In Jesus' name. Amen.

Matthew 21:1–11

A Fickle Crowd

Props Needed
A long piece of ticker tape or a long strip of paper from an adding machine
A palm branch
A palm branch for each child (optional)

The Message
Have you ever heard of a ticker-tape parade? It is a special kind of parade that takes place in New York City. The parade is usually very short, sometimes with only one person riding in it. But a ticker-tape parade is very exciting anyway. It is New York's way of honoring heroes. The special person or people ride down the street in a convertible, a car with no top. From the high windows of the tall buildings on either side of the street, people throw confetti and ticker tape. Ticker tape is a long strip of paper that looks like this. (*Show your prop.*) When the ticker tape floats down from the high windows, it looks like streamers. People line the streets, clapping and shouting 'hooray' for the people honored in the parade.

Some people who have been honored in ticker-tape parades are Neil Armstrong, the first person to walk on the moon, and Charles Lindbergh, the first person to fly an airplane across the Atlantic Ocean by himself. The New York Mets baseball team was given a surprise ticker-tape parade after they won the 1969 World Series. And ticker tape was showered on General Schwarzkopf when he came home after the war in the Persian Gulf in 1991.

Jesus was given something like a ticker-tape parade the last time he went to the city of Jerusalem before his death. Buildings weren't very tall back then, and there wasn't any ticker tape, either. But as Jesus came near Jerusalem on a donkey, the people heard about his arrival. They stood on both sides of the street as he entered the city, tore palm branches from nearby trees, and waved them in the air. (*Wave palm branch.*) They shouted, "Hooray! God bless him who comes in the name of the Lord! Praise be to God!" (NEV).

The people threw the palm branches and their coats on the road in front of Jesus' donkey so it would have a smooth path on which to walk. They cheered and gave Jesus a hero's welcome. But the crowd's love for Jesus didn't last very long.

Later that same week, the religious leaders had him arrested. Jesus was beaten and taken to the governor, Pontius Pilate. They wanted Pilate to have Jesus crucified on a cross, but Pilate couldn't find anything that Jesus had done wrong. Even so, the religious leaders, called 'pharisees,' kept telling Pilate they wanted Jesus dead.

So Pilate brought a murderer named Barabbas out of prison. A crowd was gathered outside the governor's palace. Pilate took Barabbas and Jesus and showed them to the crowd. He asked the people, "Who should I set free—Barabbas or Jesus?"

And the crowd answered, "Barabbas," even though he was a known murderer.

"Then what should I do with Jesus?" Pilate asked.

The same crowd that had welcomed Jesus as a hero a few days before now answered, "Crucify him! Crucify him!"

And so Pilate set Barabbas the murderer free and had his soldiers nail Jesus, the child of God, to a cross.

That is not the end of the story, though. I will tell you the rest next Sunday.

Let's Pray. Dear God, thank you for sending us your only child, Jesus, who showed us your way, suffered, and even died for our sakes. We are truly grateful. Amen.

Season of Easter

The Light That Never Goes Out

Prop Needed
A trick birthday candle that relights after it has been blown out

A match

The Message
Last week, we celebrated Palm Sunday and remembered Jesus' joyful parade into Jerusalem. The people greeted him as their hero, laying their coats and palm branches along his path.

Many things happened to Jesus during the time between his parade into Jerusalem and the event we celebrate this morning, most of them very sad. Remember that the religious leaders, the pharisees and priests, were getting more and more worried about Jesus. Jesus was becoming too popular with the people. And he always made the pharisees and priests out to be the bad guys in his stories. They were very jealous of him and plotted against Jesus. It was during this week that they finally put their plan into action.

On Thursday evening, Jesus had a special dinner with his twelve disciples. It was a holiday called Passover. During the Passover meal, Jesus told his disciples that one of them would turn against him and betray him. Do you know who that disciple was? (*Pause for answers.*) Judas, that's right. Judas left the party before it was over.

After dinner, Jesus and his disciples went to a garden called the Garden of Gethsemane. Jesus knew he would face some tough times in the days ahead, and he prayed to God for strength. When he finished praying a large crowd came into the garden. The people were carrying swords and clubs, and some of them were solders. At the front of the mob was Jesus' own disciple, Judas. Judas kissed Jesus to let the soldiers know which one he was. The soldiers arrested Jesus on the spot, and took him to the council of priests.

Jesus was given an unfair trial. Witnesses told the priests lies against Jesus, and the priests found him guilty of blasphemy, which means working or saying things against God. This was strange because his whole life Jesus had worked for, not against, God.

The priests took Jesus to Pilate, and asked him to put Jesus to death. We talked about Pilate, Jesus, the crowd, and Barabbas last week. Pilate asked the people what they wanted. Do you remember what they said? They wanted Barabbas the criminal set free and Jesus crucified.

Pilate gave the people what they wanted. He gave the order to his soldiers. Jesus and several criminals were nailed to crosses outside the city. Finally he died, his body was laid in a tomb, and a huge stone was rolled over the opening to the tomb. Jesus' friends were very sad. God's chosen one (*light the candle*), the light of the world, was dead. (*Blow out candle.*)

But then, something totally unexpected happened, something wonderful and miraculous. (*If the candle has not relit by now, wait until it does.*) Jesus was resurrected to new life. Here's what happened.

Three days after his death, two of Jesus' friends, both of them named Mary, went to the tomb. Suddenly, the ground shook with a huge earthquake. An angel came down from heaven, rolled the stone away, and sat on it.

The angel said, "You must not be afraid. Jesus is not here; he has been raised to new life."

The women quickly left the tomb, feeling afraid and very happy at the same time. On their way home, Jesus himself met them. He told them not to be afraid. He said he would meet the disciples in Galilee.

Jesus' story seemed sad for a while, but it had a happy ending after all. The happy ending of Jesus' life on earth is called 'resurrection.' His resurrection wasn't an ending, but the beginning of new life. But Jesus' resurrection still isn't the end of the story. Because of Jesus' resurrection, our lives can have happy endings and new beginnings, too. Jesus promises new life to everyone who believes in him. Because Jesus died for us and was resurrected, we are given the gift of new, everlasting life. The new life *of* Jesus, and our new life *in* Jesus, is what we celebrate this Easter morning.

Let's Pray. Dear God, when things seem the darkest and worst, help us to remember that there is always hope. Thank you for the new life you give to us in Jesus, and for the promise that resurrection brings. Amen.

I Doubt It

Props and Preparation Needed

Two true and one false statements about yourself, written individually on 3 × 5 cards. Write *T* or *F* in the corner of the appropriate cards. Choose things that would be of interest to children and that they probably don't know about you already

The Message

This morning we're going to start by playing a game called "I Doubt It." I'm going to tell you three things about myself. Two of the things are true, and one is not true. You have to try and figure out which of the three things is not true—or false. I will read all three things first. Then I will read each statement, one at a time. If you think a particular statement is true, don't do anything. If you think it's false, then say, "I doubt it." You are only allowed to say "I doubt it" once. The people who guess right win the game. Ready. Here we go. (*Play the game as described. At the end, reveal which statements are true and which are false by showing the* T *or* F *in the corners of the cards.*)

That's a fun game, isn't it? After playing that game, you probably have a good idea of what it means to doubt something. Doubting is when you don't believe that something is true. Sometimes we are correct when we doubt. Those of you who didn't believe that I'd met President Bush were correct, for example. But other times we doubt things that are actually true, like those of you who doubted that I ate raw eggs for breakfast or that I used to work at Disneyland. Our story this morning is about one of Jesus' disciples who doubted something that was true. Today he is still known as 'doubting Thomas.'

The story begins on the evening of the day Jesus was resurrected, the evening of the first Easter. The disciples were locked in an apartment or house, hiding. The women had told them that Jesus was raised from death, but the disciples were still afraid that the people who had Jesus killed would come after them next. All of the disciples were together except Judas, who had betrayed Jesus, and Thomas.

All of a sudden, Jesus was standing in the room. "Peace be with you," he told his disciples. He showed them the scars on his hands and his side from being nailed on the cross and stabbed with the sword, then told them to stop hiding. They were to keep doing the work of God that Jesus had started—teaching, preaching, healing, and helping others. He gave them the gift of the Holy Spirit to help them carry on that work, and then he left.

When Thomas came back, the other disciples were very excited, and they told him about Jesus' surprise visit. But Thomas didn't believe them. He doubted. "Unless I touch his scars for myself, I will not believe," he said.

A week later, the disciples were together again. This time Thomas was with them. Again Jesus came and stood in the room with them. Again he said, "Peace be with you." He walked up to Thomas and told him to touch the scars on his hands and side. "Do not doubt. Believe," Jesus said.

Thomas touched Jesus' scars and finally believed. "My Lord and my God," he said.

Jesus answered him, "Do you have to see me to believe? How happy are those who believe even though they can't see me."

Jesus wasn't angry at Thomas for doubting, just a little disappointed maybe. But Jesus did say that those who believed even though they couldn't see him or touch his scars would be blessed and very happy. We are those blessed and happy people.

Let's Pray. Dear God, we believe in Jesus even though we don't see him like the disciples did. Thank you for the special blessing of faith. In Jesus' name we pray. Amen.

THIRD SUNDAY OF EASTER   Communion
Luke 24:13–35

The Long Road
to Emmaus

Prop Needed
A whole loaf of unsliced bread

The Message
Today's story again takes place the night of Jesus' resurrection.
Two of Jesus' followers were going from the city of Jerusalem to a
village called Emmaus. It was a seven-mile walk. That would be
like walking from our church to _____. (*Choose a
well-known place that is seven miles from your church.*) That's a
long way, isn't it?

The walk seemed even longer to Jesus' friends that day because they were very sad. Have you ever noticed that when you're
sad, it's hard to move fast? Jesus' followers were very sad because
they had been in Jerusalem when Jesus was arrested. They could
do nothing but watch as their friend was being unfairly judged
and put to death. They had heard the news about the empty
tomb, but they did not understand or believe that Jesus, who was
dead, was now alive. So the two trudged along, talking quietly
with each other about all the horrible things that happened to
Jesus the week before.

While they were walking, someone came and started to walk
with them. It was Jesus, but they did not recognize him. He
asked them what they were talking about.

The two stopped walking. They stood frozen with sad faces. One
of them, named Cleopas, asked Jesus, "Are you the only visitor in
Jerusalem who doesn't know what has happened there in the
past few days?"

"What things?" Jesus asked.

"The things that happened to Jesus of Nazareth," they answered. "This man was special. He was a prophet, and was powerful in everything he said and did. Our religious leaders were

jealous of him, and had him arrested. He was crucified. And we had hoped that he would be the one sent by God to free Israel." Then they explained the confusing news about the women going to the tomb and finding it empty.

Jesus listened to all they said. Then he said to them, "You are so foolish and slow to believe!" He told them that God's chosen messiah had to suffer all those things, even to die, before he could return to heaven. He explained all the Scriptures to them and how Jesus died for the sins of all people so that they could live with God and Jesus in heaven someday, too. The stranger really seemed to know what he was talking about.

The three came to Emmaus late in the afternoon. Cleopas asked the stranger to stay with them, and so he did. While they were sitting around the supper table together, the stranger took the bread in his hands. (*Pick up your loaf.*) He said grace. (*Raise loaf.*) Then he broke the bread. (*Break loaf in half, as during communion.*) Finally, Jesus' followers recognized who he was, and then he disappeared. They were amazed that they hadn't known who he was earlier. That night, they walked all the way back to Jerusalem to tell the disciples what had happened, and how they had recognized Jesus in the breaking of the bread.

We still recognize Jesus in the breaking of the bread today. We call it 'communion,' or 'the Lord's supper.' Each month (*or however often you celebrate communion in your church*), we celebrate communion during worship. We share a taste of bread and remember Jesus' body which was broken for us. We share a sip of wine (*or grape juice*) and remember that Jesus bled for us. We remember Jesus' pain, his death, and his resurrection to new life. Communion brings us closer together as a community of faith and closer to Jesus our savior as we remember and recognize him in the breaking of the bread.

Let's Pray. Dear God, thank you for sharing your child with us in the breaking of the bread and always. In Jesus' name. Amen.

FOURTH SUNDAY OF EASTER   The Good Shepherd
John 10:1–16

A Job Well Done

Props Needed
Several people from your congregation who do different things
for a living

The Message
Three people are going to share our time together this morning. You might recognize them. That is because Mr. Joseph, Ms.
Kyle, and Ms. Kelleher are all members of our church. Each one
of them works at a different job during the week. They are going
to tell us a little bit about what their jobs are and why they like
them. Let's start with Mr. Joseph. (*Have guests tell briefly about
their work and why they like it.*)

Thank you very much for sharing with us about your work.
Those are all important and interesting jobs. Boys and girls, do
you ever think about what you'd like to be when you grow up?
What jobs do you want to have? (*Listen to answers.*) Those are all
important and interesting jobs, too. I hope that whatever work
you choose, you will do the very best job you can.

Unfortunately, not all people try their best at their jobs. There
are people who do a good job and people who do a poor job in every type of work. There are good gardeners and sloppy gardeners,
good waiters and rude ones. Some photographers take great pictures, others not so great.

A well-known type of worker in Bible times was the shepherd.
We don't hear much about shepherds today, but there were many
shepherds back then. A shepherd's job was to take care of sheep.
We've talked about shepherds before. The shepherd made sure
there was enough food and water for the sheep. Before the shepherd took the flock of sheep to a new pasture to eat, he or she
cleared the pasture of any poisonous weeds or thorns. The shepherd also got rid of any dangerous snakes and scorpions that
might harm the sheep. The shepherd protected the sheep from
wild animals and also from people who might try to steal them. If
a sheep wandered off and got lost, the shepherd looked for it and
found it.

There were good shepherds and bad shepherds. The best shepherds were those who took good care of their sheep, not just because it was a job, but because they loved the sheep.

Jesus called himself 'the good shepherd.' He called us his sheep. Jesus cares for us and protects us. He watches over us and helps us. Most of all, Jesus loves us. Jesus is the good shepherd who takes excellent care of his sheep, who are you, me, and all those who follow him.

Let's Pray. Dear God, thank you for Jesus, the good shepherd, who watches over and takes good care of us. And thank you for these precious children. Amen.

FIFTH SUNDAY OF EASTER   Jesus as Way to God
John 14:1–14

Finding Your Way

Prop Needed
A compass

The Message
This morning, I have a special instrument, or tool, to show you. It's called a compass. A compass is used by people who want to know which direction they're going—north, south, east, or west. Navigators on ships and airplanes use compasses to keep their ships and planes on course. Hikers also use compasses to keep from getting lost.

Let's pretend we're in the woods. All around us are tall trees. We're going hiking, and we have our trusty compass with us. Let's begin our hike over here. Follow me. (*Lead group to the base of one of the sanctuary aisles.*) We want to go in this direction. (*Point down aisle.*) When we stand here and look in the direction we want to go, the needle on the compass points to *N.* Can you all see it? (*Show children the compass reading.*) When we hike in that direction, we will be heading north. Let's try it. Would you like to hold the compass? (*Hand the compass to one of the children and walk down the aisle. At the end of the aisle, stay facing the same direction.*) Imagine that we've been hiking for half an hour. What does the needle on the compass point to now? (*Help child read the compass, if necessary.*) It is still pointing to *N.* We've been hiking north all this time!

Now we want to get back to our camp. Does anyone have any ideas on how we might do that? (*Listen to answers.*) We could just turn around and start walking, but with all the tall trees between here and camp, I'm afraid we might get lost. We need something to show us the way. Did I hear someone say we could use the compass? That's an excellent idea!

Everyone turn around. Look at the compass now. Where is the needle pointing now? To the *S,* which stands for south. South is the opposite direction from north. If we walk south, we should

64

end up where we started. Let's go! Let's keep checking the compass as we walk, to make sure we are always walking south.

(*Seated again.*) So that's how a compass can help you find your way in the woods.

Once, when Jesus was talking to his disciples, he told them how they could find their way to God, and it wasn't by using a compass. Jesus said, "I am the way, the truth, and the life." Jesus told his disciples that the way to find God was through him. He said that if they knew Jesus, then they already knew God, because God was in Jesus, and Jesus was in God. God and Jesus are one God.

When we learn about Jesus, then we learn about God. The more we know about what God is like, the more we know about Jesus. The closer we get to Jesus as our friend, the closer we get to God. Jesus is the compass pointing us in the direction of God. Jesus is the way to God, the truth about God, and the life everlasting with God.

Let's Pray. Dear God, thank you for sending us your child Jesus to show us the way to you, to teach us what you are truly like, and to make life everlasting possible for us. Amen.

Mirror, Mirror, on the Wall

Prop Needed
A mirror

The Message

(*Hold mirror up to children so they can see themselves.*) When you look in this mirror, what do you see? (*Pause for answers.*) You see yourself, right. When you look in a mirror, you are looking at what we call your 'reflection.' You can also see your reflection by looking in a shiny glass window or a still pond.

When people look at you, do they ever tell you that you look like one of your parents or grandparents? I was always told that I looked like my father. "Oh, you have your father's dark eyes," people would say. My little boy looks like me, so he looks like his grandfather, too. (*Use your own example.*) When a baby is born, people always try to figure out who she or he looks like—the mother or the father. (*Point to a child.*) I think you look like your mother. Has anyone ever told you that? What about the rest of you? Have you ever been told that you look like someone? (*Listen to answers.*) What's funny is when one person says, "You look exactly like your father," and then the next week someone else says, "You look exactly like your mother."

When you look like one of your parents or grandparents, that person is reflected in you. Just as when you look in a mirror and see your own reflection, when people look at you, they see your mom or dad reflected in your eyes or your smile.

We can be reflections of others in the ways we think and act, too. If your mom likes gardening and you like to work in the garden too, then your mother's love of gardening is reflected in you, even if you don't look a thing like her. If your dad is a kind person and you are kind to others as well, then we could say that your father's kindness is reflected in you. We can also reflect qualities we find in people other than our parents. We can be reflections of qualities we find in older brothers or sisters, other relatives, friends, even people we look up to on TV, in sports, or from history.

There is one person that all of you reflect. Even though you have different parents, live in different families, and have different heroes, all of you are God's children. Each and every one of you is a reflection of God's love.

When you are kind or loving, when you are generous and share what you have with others, when you play the game your friend wants to play instead of insisting on having your own way, when you are helpful to your parents—you are sharing the love of God that is within your heart. You are a reflection of God's love.

God put the love in your heart by giving you a special gift. When Jesus was about to leave his disciples, he promised them that God would send another helper so that they would not be all alone. That helper is the Holy Spirit. God sent the Holy Spirit to live in the hearts of Jesus' followers, to give them what they needed to carry on Jesus' work in the world. Jesus' followers still have the gift of the Holy Spirit today. you have the love of God in your heart because you and all God's children have been given the gift of the Holy Spirit.

So when people look at you (*hold up mirror and pan group so they can see themselves as you speak and use their names*), they see Kathy or Dennis or Elise. And they might also see your mother's hair, your grandfather's nose, or your dad's interest in model trains. When people see you, they will also see the love of God, because you are a reflection of that love.

Let's Pray. Dear God, thank you for making us who we are. Thank you for the gift of your Holy Spirit. May we be reflections of your love in everything we do. Amen.

On Helping Others

Prop Needed
An article from your denominational magazine describing a mission project of your church (with pictures, if possible). Adapt the story to match your article

The Message
This morning I want to share with you an article I read this past week. The article came from our church magazine, *Presbyterian Survey*. It's about one of the mission projects our church works with in Africa. (*Describe the project. Focus on how important the work is and how much it helps the people it serves. Show any pictures accompanying the article.*)

Isn't that a great project? I get a good feeling knowing that our church is working with people in Africa so they can have enough food to eat. You know, when we give money to the church each week, part of that money goes to help with mission projects like this one. We may have helped to pay for seeds that were planted or tools that the farmers use. Giving money is one way we can help the church do God's work in the world. This work seems so important, though. I wish we could do more than just give money, don't you?

We could all buy plane tickets and fly to Africa this afternoon! Then we could help to plant the seeds, harvest the grain, and get the food to the people who need it. Oh, but some of you have to go to school tomorrow, don't you? I'll bet your parents wouldn't let you go, anyway. Besides, it sounds like they already have enough people to do the work.

Well, what else could we do to help? I know! We could spread the word. We could tell the rest of the people in the church about the great work we're doing to stop hunger in Africa. (*Look out at the congregation.*) Have you folks heard about Project Food? Oh, they've heard already. They must have been listening when I was telling you about it.

Can you think of anything else we might be able to do to help Project Food? (*Listen to answers.*) We can pray for Project Food, can't we? Praying for other people is a very important part of our work as Christians.

We can pray for anyone who needs help. When people are sick or in need of things like food or a place to live, when they are lonely or afraid, we can pray and ask God to be with them and help them. Sometimes just knowing that someone else cares enough about us to pray for us makes us feel better. We can pray for people we know and for people we don't know. God listens to our prayers either way. When we pray for other people, it is called 'intercessory' prayer.

Let's Pray. Dear God, thank you for the work our church is doing with the hungry in Africa. Be with the people who work with Project Food. Be with the hungry people who need the food that the project grows. Help us all to work for a fair world where everyone gets enough to eat and no one is hungry. In Jesus' name. Amen.

1 Corinthians 12:3b–13

God's Tool Box

Props Needed
An assortment of hand tools in a paper bag or tool box

The Message
Before coming to church this morning, I went to my workbench in the garage and picked up several things to show you. Here's the first thing. (*Hold up a hammer.*) Does anyone recognize what this is? (*Pause for answers.*) A hammer, that's right. What is a hammer used for? (*Pause.*) Yes, you hammer nails with it. You might hammer a nail into the wall to hang a picture, or you might hammer boards together to build a table, some shelves, or even a house. What about this thing? What is it? (*Pause.*) A screwdriver, right. This is used for putting things together with screws. I once used a screwdriver to hang up curtain rods. Let's see what other stuff I brought. What's this? A saw. You cut wood to the size you need with a saw. Here's something strange looking. Does anyone know what this is? (*Pause.*) It's a plane. You run this along rough wood to make it smooth and straight. I also have a level, which is used to make sure whatever you are building is level to the ground and not tipped to one side or the other.

So, we have a hammer, a screwdriver, a saw, a plane, and a level. Each one of these things is different. Each one does a different job, doesn't it? But all these different things have something in common, too. When you put hem all together in a group, what are they called? (*Pause for answers.*) They are all tools, aren't they? When these tools work together in the hands of a skilled carpenter, they can be used to build beautiful, strong, magnificent projects.

The church is like these tools. Each person in the church is different. We each have our own skills and abilities. Each one of us in the church has a different job to do. Some of us are teachers, some leaders, some ushers, some singers. Some of us are good listeners, and some are good at letting other people know that we care about them. Some of us are good cooks, and some are good eaters, as you probably know from coming to church dinners. Some of us are good helpers, some good cleaner-uppers, some good thinkers, some good preachers, some good smilers. God has given each of us a special job to do in the church.

Like the hammer, screwdriver, and saw, we also have something in common with each other. We are all part of the family of God. Together with God's children everywhere, we are the Church.

Before Jesus started his ministry as a preacher, he worked as a carpenter. Sometimes Jesus is called the 'master carpenter' because he is the head of the Church. Jesus the master carpenter directs all of us as we work together on the project of building the Reign of God.

Let's Pray. Dear God, we thank you for each adult and child here and for the talent he or she brings to the work of the church. Even more than that, we thank you for each person's love and friendship. In the name of Jesus the Christ and master carpenter. Amen.

Season after Pentecost

Getting a Clear Picture

Props Needed
A three-legged camera tripod with removable or adjustable legs
A camera loaded with film

The Message
Good morning. Have any of you seen one of these before? (*Show your assembled tripod.*) It is called a tripod. Does anyone know what a tripod is used for? (*Pause for answers.*) A tripod is used to hold a camera. The tripod holds the camera very still while the photographer takes a picture. The tripod helps make the picture turn out clear, rather than blurry, by holding the camera still. Another time you might use a tripod is when you, the photographer, want to be in the picture yourself. You put the camera on the tripod, push a timer button on the camera, run around to be in the picture, and the camera snaps the picture itself.

So a tripod is used to hold a camera. Does anyone know why it is called a tripod? (*Pause.*) It's called a tripod because it has three legs. In Greek, *tri* means three, and *pod* means foot. So, *tripod* means 'three-footed' or 'three legs.' How many wheels does a tricycle have? (*Pause.*) How many sides does a triangle have? (*Pause.*) How many legs does a tripod have? (*Pause.*) Why do you think a tripod has three legs? (*Pause for answers.*) It takes three legs to hold up the camera, doesn't it?

If you were to remove one leg from the tripod or make one leg shorter than the others (*remove or shorten one leg*), the camera won't stay up, will it? (*Try to set up lopsided tripod. Catch it as it falls.*) You need three legs that are the same length to hold up the camera. Each leg is as important as the other two. Without all three equal legs, the tripod is not complete. It cannot do its job.

God is like this tripod. We worship one God. But God is made up of three equal parts. We believe in God, who created the world and everything and everyone in it. We also believe in Jesus who came to earth to teach us about God, to show us how much God loves us, and to save us from our sin. And we believe in God the Holy Spirit, who lives in our hearts and helps us in our work as Christians.

There is one God with three parts, just like one tripod has three legs. And like the legs of this tripod, each part of God is just as important as the others. Without all three equal parts—Father, Son, and Holy Spirit—God is not complete.

God, Christ, and the Holy Spirit are called the 'trinity.' The word *trinity* starts with the letters *T-R-I, tri,* just like tripod, triangle, and tricycle. That's because the trinity is God, three-in-one. Only by knowing all three—God, Christ, and Holy Spirit—can we get a clear picture of God.

To end our time together, I want to put this tripod to the test by taking our picture. Everybody bunch together. (*Set up the camera on the tripod, push the time release button, and run around and get in the picture yourself.*) Say "Trinity!" (*Next Sunday, bring the snapshot to show the children.*)

Moving Day

Prop Needed

A large cardboard carton, preferably with the name of a moving company printed on it

The Message

Have any of you ever moved from one home to another? Have you had someone new move into your neighborhood from someplace else? Moving can be fun and exciting. You get to meet new people, make new friends, and explore a new neighborhood.

But some parts of moving are not very much fun. Getting ready to move is a lot of work. You have to pack all your things into boxes like this one. (*Show the carton.*) Sometimes when people move, they use a moving company. Workers from the moving company come and get all the people's things and put them into a big truck. Then the movers drive the truck to the new home and unload all the stuff. After that comes the big job of unpacking the boxes and putting everything away again.

Another hard thing about moving is saying good-bye to friends in your old neighborhood. Living in a new place can be kind of scary at first.

One day a long, long time ago, God asked a man named Abraham to move. God asked Abraham to pack up his wife, Sarah, and his nephew, Lot, his servants, and everything he owned, and move to a place he had never seen before. God had very special plans for Abraham and Sarah.

We think moving is hard today, but for Abraham and Sarah it was even harder. There were no moving trucks in those days. They had to load their stuff onto camels. The land they had to travel across was hot, dry desert. Abraham didn't know whether his new neighbors would be friendly or not. He and his family might move to the new land and be killed by the people who already lived there. On top of all that, Abraham was seventy-five years old.

It was a scary thing the Lord had asked Abraham to do, but he and Sarah trusted God. God promised to be with them on their journey to the new land and always. So they went. They packed up everything, loaded it on camels, gathered their nephew and servants together, and set off across the desert. They didn't know where they were going, but they trusted God to get them there safely. And that's exactly what God did.

Let's Pray. Dear God, we thank you for always being with us, just like you were with Abraham and Sarah. Help us to have the same kind of strong, trusting faith that they had. Amen.

THIRD SUNDAY AFTER PENTECOST   Proper 5
Genesis 22:1–18   Abraham Nearly Sacrifices Isaac

Sacrificing for God

Prop Needed
  An offering plate

The Message
  Last week we talked about a man named Abraham and how
God asked him to do something very difficult. Do you remember
what that thing was? (*Pause for answers.*) That's right. God asked
Abraham to move with his wife Sarah to a place they had never
seen before. This morning's story is about Abraham too, and
something God asked him to do that was even harder than moving to a foreign land.
  God promised Abraham many descendants. That means lots of
grandchildren, great-grandchildren, and so on. But Abraham
and Sarah were getting very old, and they didn't have any children yet. Finally, when Abraham was one hundred years old, his
wife Sarah had a baby boy. They named him Isaac, and he was
very precious to them.
  A few years later, God spoke to Abraham. God told him to take
his only child, Isaac, to a special mountain and offer him as a sacrifice to God there.
  Abraham and his people often sacrificed animals to show their
love to God. They would kill an animal and burn it on a special
stone table called an altar. They believed that animal sacrifices
made God happy. They never sacrificed people, though, especially
not children. Yet this seemed to be what God wanted Abraham
to do.
  Early the next morning, Abraham cut some wood, loaded it on
his donkey, and left home with Isaac. They walked for three days
until they finally came to the mountain. Now, Isaac knew that he
and his father had come to this place to offer a sacrifice to God,
but he had no idea that the sacrifice was to be him. He said to his
dad, "The fire and the wood are here, but where is the lamb for

the burnt offering?" Abraham said, "God himself will provide the lamb for a burnt offering."

Abraham built an altar at the place God had told him about. He put the wood on top if it, then he put Isaac on top of the wood. He had already picked up the knife to kill Isaac when he heard a voice call, "Abraham! Abraham!"

"Here I am," he said.

Then the voice told him not to hurt his son after all. Abraham looked around and saw a ram caught by his horns in a bush. He caught the ram and offered it as an offering instead of his son.

Today we don't believe in burnt sacrifices. We don't believe that killing animals or people makes God happy. But we do give offerings to show our love to the Lord. (*Show offering plates.*) We give money during the offering time in church, don't we? We also give part of our time and talents to God when we help other people. Sharing who we are and what we have with others makes God very happy.

Let's Pray. God, we do love you. Help us to live in a way that shows you just how much by giving and sharing with others. Amen.

Brotherly "Love"

Prop Needed
None

The Message

How many of you are only children—with no brothers or sisters? If you have brothers and sisters, raise your hand. How many of you are the youngest child in your family? If you are a middle child, with brothers or sisters older or younger than you, raise your hand.

Are all kids in a family exactly alike? Do they always look exactly alike? Do all the children in a family like to do exactly the same things? Of course not! You might have curly hair and blue eyes, while your brother has straight hair and brown eyes. You might like to play the tuba, while your sister likes to play soccer. All people are different, even if they belong to the same family. That is what makes each one of us special.

This morning I want to tell you about two brothers, Jacob and Esau. They were the sons of Isaac and his wife, Rebecca. We talked about Isaac last week. Jacob and Esau were twins, but you couldn't find two more different people anywhere.

Esau was born first, so he was the oldest. He had lots of red hair, not only on his head, but all over! Esau grew up to be a hunter and liked the out-of-doors. His younger brother, Jacob, wasn't as hairy as Esau. He grew up to be a quiet man who liked to stay home.

Now let me ask you some more questions. Do you always get along with your brothers and sisters? Do you always share everything and treat each other with kindness like your parents say you should? Jacob and Esau didn't get along well at all. They fought all the time and sometimes didn't seem to like each other very much.

One day when Jacob was cooking some bean soup, Esau came in from hunting, and he was very hungry. He asked Jacob if he could have some of the soup because he was starving. Instead of sharing the soup generously as he should have, Jacob made Esau buy it from him. Jacob told Esau he could have some soup if he let Jacob have his rights as the first-born son.

In those days, the oldest boy in a family was treated as the most important just because he had been born first. This was called a 'birthright.' Jacob was tired of being treated second best and wanted to be given the special treatment that his brother had. So when he saw how hungry Esau was, he took unfair advantage of his big brother and made him trade his birthright for a lousy bowl of soup. Esau was so hungry that he forgot how important his birthright was and agreed to the trade.

Today we know that every child is special and just as important as the other members of the family. It doesn't matter whether you're the oldest, middle, youngest, or an only child. Your parents love you and God loves you just for your being you.

Let's Pray. Dear God, we thank you for giving us our families, even if we don't always get along as well as we would like. Amen.

Heirs of the Promise

Prop Needed

A picture of your grandparents or great-grandparents

The Message

Good morning. Today I have a very old picture to show you. This is a picture of my great-great-grandparents and their children. See the gentleman sitting in the front? He is my mother's father's father. And the little boy standing next to him is my great-grandfather. These people are my ancestors, and we are all related. Even though the people in this picture died a long time ago, we are still members of the same family. (*Your description should, of course, reflect your own family situation.*)

You and I are members of the same family, too. Does that surprise you? The family we share isn't exactly like the family you live with and go on vacations with. But you and I and every person in this sanctuary all belong to the same large family. I am talking about the family of God.

As members of God's family, we share some of the same ancestors. Abraham is one of our ancestors in the family of God. Thousands of years ago, God made a very important promise to Abraham. God promised Abraham a land his family could live in and call their own. God promised to always be with Abraham and his family. And God promised Abraham so many descendants that he wouldn't be able to count them all. That means lots of grandchildren and great-grandchildren.

Abraham's first descendant was his son, Isaac. God then passed the promise on from Isaac to Jacob. The promise was then passed to Jacob's twelve sons, who passed it on to their children, and so on, until today the promise is passed on to us. We are members of the family of God because we believe and trust in God's promise to always be with us.

The most powerful way God has kept the promise is by sending Jesus into the world. Because Jesus died and rose again to new life, we know that nothing can separate us, keep us apart, from God.

Remember I said that the promise was passed from Isaac to Jacob? This is kind of hard to understand because Jacob was the sneaky guy we talked about last week. He stole the birthright from his brother Esau by trading a bowl of soup for it.

I think it's important to know that God's promises aren't only for people who are always good. I don't know anyone who is good all the time, do you? God promises to love and stand by all of us, even when we aren't perfect, even when we make mistakes. After all, that's what family is for.

Let's Pray. Dear God, thank you for welcoming us into your family. In the name of Jesus, we pray. Amen.

Genesis 32:22–32   Jacob at Peniel

Learning the Hard Way

Props Needed
None

The Message

Do any of you ever roughhouse or wrestle with your brothers or sisters, with a friend, or with your mom or dad? I used to wrestle with my best friend, Billy. Billy and I used to tumble around on the grass until one of us pinned the other person's arms down. Then the person on the bottom had to say a special word before getting up. Can you guess what that word was? (*Pause for answers.*) Uncle! The person on the bottom could get up only when he or she cried "uncle," and we'd go play something else together. It was a fun game. (*Adapt the story to fit your childhood experience, or ask the children what the loser has to say before the winner lets him or her go when they wrestle.*) Our story this morning is about Jacob and an unusual wrestling match he was once in.

Jacob was on his way back home. Years before, he had left his home because he was afraid that his brother Esau was going to kill him. Jacob had been pretty rotten to Esau, and Esau was furious when Jacob left. While he was away, Jacob got married, had children, and became quite rich. Finally he decided that it was time to return home and face his brother. He sent a messenger ahead with a polite note to Esau. He sent his brother gifts. Then he sent his family, his servants, and all his livestock—sheep, goats, and cattle—ahead of him, and he spent the night alone by a river. But he didn't get any sleep.

Just as Jacob was settling down for the night, someone came and wrestled with him. They fought all night long. This was no game. Just before the sun came up, the stranger could tell he was losing. He hit Jacob on the hip (*point to your hip*), and it went out of joint. That is kind of like breaking, but not as bad. It still hurts, though. But Jacob didn't let go.

The stranger asked Jacob to let him go because the sun was coming up. Jacob said, "I won't let you go unless you bless me." In a way, that was like asking the man to 'cry uncle.' It was admitting that he had lost the fight. But a blessing would be more, too. When you give a blessing to someone, you wish them well or pray that good things will happen to them.

The stranger asked Jacob what his name was. Then he said, "I am changing your name to Israel, which means 'he struggles with God,' because you have struggled with God and with people, and won."

Jacob asked the stranger his name, but the stranger wouldn't tell him. Then he blessed Jacob and left. When the stranger was gone, Jacob finally realized who he was. The person Jacob had been wrestling with all night was God.

Jacob's nightlong struggle with God changed him. He received a new name, Israel, but he also became a new person. When they finally met the next day, Esau forgave Jacob for all the rotten things he had done, and the two brothers finally became friends. Wrestling with God was a hard thing to do, but Jacob didn't give up. In the end, he was blessed and became a better person for his struggle.

Let's Pray. Dear God, we thank you for our ancestors in the faith who teach us how to be your children, not only when it's easy, but also when it's hard. Amen.

Cruisin' Down the River

Props Needed
   Flannel board
   Flannel-board figures (found in the Appendix)

The Message
   For several weeks, we have talked about Jacob. Today we're going to finish Jacob's story and find out what happens to his family next.
   Jacob returned home to the land of Canaan after making up with his brother, Esau. Jacob had twelve sons. A terrible famine came to Canaan. Do you know what a famine is? (*Pause for answers.*) Right. A famine is when something happens to the crops, and there isn't enough food to eat. Jacob and his family moved to another country called Egypt. In Egypt there was enough food, and Jacob's family was treated well.
   The family grew and grew until there were seventy people in it! They were called Hebrews. Jacob and his family, the Hebrews, all believed in God and the promises God had made to Abraham and Sarah, to Isaac and Rebecca, and to Jacob and Rachel. The Hebrews were God's special people.
   As time went on, Jacob grew old and died. So did his twelve sons and their wives. But the Hebrew people had more and more babies and grew stronger and stronger. A new king came to power in Egypt. In Egypt, the king is called the 'pharaoh.' The new pharaoh became worried about the Hebrews. There were so many of them that he was afraid of what might happen if they ever decided to turn against him. So he made the Hebrews his slaves. He forced them to work very hard for him. The Hebrews built fabulous cities out of huge, heavy stones. They worked in the pharaoh's fields under the hot sun. But this unkind treatment did

not discourage the Hebrews. They continued to get married and have more babies.

The pharaoh told the midwives who helped the Hebrew women give birth to kill all the boy babies that were born. But the midwives believed in God and would not kill the babies. Finally, the pharaoh ordered that all Hebrew boy babies were to be thrown in the Nile River. Isn't that terrible?

One day, a Hebrew couple had a baby boy. His mother hid him for three months. But as he grew he got louder, and it became impossible to hide him any longer. So she wove a special basket and painted the inside with tar so it would float. She put the baby in the basket. (*Show flannel-board figure of basket with baby inside. Have reeds and river in place on flannel board.*) Then she went to the Nile River and gently placed the basket in the tall grass at the edge of the water. (*Place the basket among the reeds. Follow the story from this point with flannel-board figures.*) The baby's older sister hid nearby and watched to see what would happen.

Before long, the pharaoh's daughter came to the river to take a bath. She saw the basket in the tall grass and asked one of her servants to get it for her. When she opened the basket, the princess found a baby boy. He was crying. "This is one of the Hebrew babies," she said.

Then the baby's sister stepped forward and said, "Would you like me to get one of the Hebrew women to nurse and take care of the baby for you?" The princess said, "Yes, please." So the girl brought the baby's own mother to the princess. The baby's mother worked for the princess, taking care of the baby. The princess adopted the baby as her own son and named him . . . does anybody know? Moses.

Moses grew up to be a very important person who helped God and the Hebrews. It's important to remember that Moses wouldn't have lived to help if it were not for the cleverness of his mother and the kindness of the princess.

Let's Pray. Dear God, we thank you for the Bible and the people in it who helped carry out your plan for the world. May we be your helpful followers, too. Amen.

Troubleshooting

Props Needed
Flannel board
Flannel-board figures (found in the Appendix)

The Message
(*Have pictures of baby Moses in the basket on the flannel board.*)
Last week we talked about a baby whose mother put him into a
basket on a river to save him from an evil king, the pharaoh. The
pharaoh's daughter found the baby and rescued him. Do you remember the baby's name? (*Pause for answers.*) His name was
Moses.

The princess adopted Moses, and he grew up as her son. (*Re-
place the baby with the adult Moses figure.*) But he also knew that
he was born a Hebrew. So, even though he lived in the palace, he
saw how hard the Hebrews were forced to work. (*Place pictures of
hard-working slaves on the board.*) And how cruelly the pharaoh's
men treated them. (*Place Egyptian taskmaster on board, whip-
ping slaves.*) Moses didn't like what he saw.

One day Moses went out to visit his people. (*Follow story with
flannel-board figures.*) He watched an Egyptian kill a Hebrew
slave. Moses felt very sad and angry. He looked around to make
sure no one was looking, then he killed the Egyptian and hid his
body in the sand.

The next day Moses was walking in the same part of town
again, when he saw two Hebrew men fighting. Moses asked the
man who had started the fight why he was beating up the other
man. The man answered Moses, "Why? What are you going to do
about it? Kill me like you did that Egyptian?" Moses became very
afraid. Even though he'd tried to hide it, people knew that he had
killed the Egyptian. It wasn't long before Pharaoh heard about it,
too, and he tried to have Moses killed. Moses ran away to a country called Midian.

Moses got himself into quite a mess, didn't he? The Egyptian
was wrong to kill the Hebrew slave. But did his crime give Moses
the right to kill the Egyptian? Was Moses right to kill the Egyp-

tian? (*Pause for answers.*) If you see someone hurting another person, what should you do? If you see two kids fighting on the playground, or one child grab a toy away from another, what should you do? (*Pause for answers.*)

It's not right to turn the other way and ignore a problem when someone else isn't being treated fairly. But you shouldn't jump into the fight and start slugging away, either. You mentioned some good ways to help. Try talking to the others, and get them to stop what they're doing—fighting or grabbing toys or whatever. Or you can go get a grown-up to help straighten out the mess.

Moses got himself into a heap of trouble and had to run away to save his life. The story worked out okay in the end, even though Moses made a mistake. We'll hear more about what happened to Moses next week.

Let's Pray. Dear God, when we see someone in trouble, show us the best way to help that person. In Jesus' name. Amen.

The Burning Bush—Sort Of

Props Needed
> A charred piece of wood
> Some ashes

The Message

Have any of you ever watched a fire burn? Have you ever sat around a campfire, listening to the wood sizzle and pop as it burns? Maybe you've watched hot red sparks float up the chimney while logs burn in the fireplace below. The next day, when the fire has burned completely out, what would you find in the spot where the burning logs had been? (*Pause for answers.*) You might find some charred pieces of wood like this one. (*Show the charred wood.*) For some reason, this log didn't burn up all the way. You can see how the fire scarred the wood, though, can't you? Most of the logs in your fireplace or campfire would be gone, though, and all you'd find in their place would be ashes. (*Show the ashes.*) This morning's story is about Moses again and about a very strange fire he saw at a very special mountain.

Last week, we learned how Moses was forced to leave Egypt. He wound up living in a country called Midian. In Midian, he married a woman called Zipporah, and they had a baby boy. Moses' job was to help his wife's father, Jethro. Moses may have thought he was finished with Egypt and would never go home again, but God had a different idea.

One day, Moses was taking care of Jethro's sheep and goats. What do we call a person who cares for sheep? (*Pause for answers.*) A shepherd, right. Moses the shepherd took the flock of animals across the hot, dry desert to a mountain where there was plenty of grass for the animals to eat and water for them to drink. The mountain was called Sinai.

When Moses got to the mountain, he saw something very strange. A bush was on fire, yet it wasn't really. There were flames coming out of the bush, but it was not burning up like this piece of wood did. (*Refer to prop.*) The leaves were still green, and the bark was still fresh.

Moses had never seen anything like it before, so he walked closer to get a better look. The Bible tells us that, as Moses came close to the burning bush, he heard a voice call his name, "Moses! Moses!"

Moses answered, "Here I am."

Then the voice said, "Don't come any closer. Take off your sandals because the ground you are standing on is holy." Then the voice told Moses who was speaking. "I am the God of your ancestors. I am the God of Abraham and Sarah, of Isaac and Rebecca, of Jacob and Rachel. I have seen how cruel the Egyptians are to my people, the Hebrews. I have heard their prayers asking to be rescued from their slave drivers. And so I have come to free them from the Egyptians. I will bring them out of Egypt and take them to a land where they can make their home. Now, I want you to go to the king of Egypt and tell him to let my people go. And then I want you to lead them to this land which I have promised.

Moses didn't think he could do it. He told God, "I'm not anyone special! I'm just a shepherd! How can I go to the king and bring the people out of Egypt?"

But God knew Moses could do the job because he would not be alone. God said, "I will be with you."

Jesus once told his disciples, "For people, it is impossible, but anything is possible for God." (Mt. 19:26). We can do amazing things with God's help, things we would never be able to do on our own. Moses will learn this lesson before the story is over. We'll hear what happens next to Moses a week from now.

Let's Pray. Dear God, thank you for always being with us and for helping us to do the hard things we need to do. Amen.

What's in a Name?

Prop Needed

A book of baby names with their meanings

The Message

Good morning, boys and girls. Today we're going to begin by talking about names. Is there anyone here who does not have a name? Of course not! Everybody has a name, right? Sometimes names have a special meaning. For example, the man we discussed last week was named Moses. Moses means 'to pull out.' Pharaoh's daughter named him Moses when he was a baby, because she pulled him out of the Nile River and rescued him.

Parents today usually pick names for their babies before they are born. Sometimes they use a book like this one to help them decide on names. (*Hold up the baby name book.*) It lists hundreds and hundreds of names for boys and girls and tells what those names mean. Let's look up a few names and find out what they mean. Let's see . . . my name is Dianne. We look up 'Dianne' in the book, and find out that it means 'divine.' Daniel, let's look up your name. (*Look up several of the children's names and read their meanings.*) You probably never knew you had such interesting names.

God has a special name too. Our story today is about how Moses learns God's name.

Remember that in last week's story, God spoke to Moses from the burning bush. God asked Moses to go to the king of Egypt, the pharaoh, and lead the Hebrew people out of slavery in Egypt.

Moses was hesitant about this assignment. In fact, the longer he thought about it, the more he realized he didn't want to do it. He didn't want to be the one to help free God's people. So he gave God excuses, hoping the Lord would allow him to forget the whole idea and go back to taking care of his sheep.

Moses said, "If I go to the Hebrews and tell them, 'The God of your ancestors sent me,' they will want to know your name. What should I tell them?"

No one had ever known God's name before, so Moses may have been surprised when God answered, "My name is Yahweh, which means 'I am what I am.' " That is kind of an unusual name, isn't it? But it means something very important. God is who God is. We cannot change God or talk God into doing something God doesn't want to do. Yahweh is the same yesterday, today, and tomorrow.

Next God said to Moses, "Tell my people that Yahweh has sent you to free them from slavery and lead them into the promised land." Yahweh then told Moses that the Hebrew people would listen to him, but also warned that Pharaoh would not let the people go easily. That will be our story for next week.

Let's Pray. Dear Yahweh God, thank you for making yourself known to Moses and to us. Amen.

ELEVENTH SUNDAY AFTER PENTECOST   Proper 13
Exodus 12:1–14   The Ten Plagues

Let My People Go!

Props Needed
A songleader (could be the storyteller)
Piano or guitar accompaniment

The Message
This morning I want to tell you what happened next to Moses and God's people, the Hebrews. I'd like you to help me tell the story. We're going to learn a song. At certain points in the story, I will ask you to sing. First, let's learn the song. It's called, "Go Down, Moses." (*Teach the children the song, line by line.*)

That's great! Now we're ready to begin the story.

Last week, God asked Moses to return home to Egypt, bring the Hebrew people out of slavery, and take them to the land God had promised. Moses really wished God would choose someone else for the job, but in the end he said he would do it. So Moses took his wife, his sons, and his brother Aaron and went back to Egypt.

Moses and Aaron went before the pharaoh, the king of Egypt, and Moses told him, "The Lord, God of Israel has sent me to you. Let God's people go!" (*Sing the entire song.*)

But the pharaoh was stubborn, and he refused to let the Hebrews go. He treated them even more cruelly than before. So Moses took another message to the pharaoh.

"If you do not let the Hebrews go, then God will do terrible things to Egypt and its people. The water in the Nile River will be turned to blood. The Egyptians and their animals will not be able to drink the water. The Lord says, 'Let my people go!' (*Sing the last two lines of the song.*)

The Nile River turned to blood, but still the pharaoh wouldn't let the Hebrews go. Moses went back to him and said, "If you do not let the Hebrews go, then God will sent thousands of frogs to Egypt. Frogs will be in the Nile, in your homes, in your beds, even in your pots and pans! The Lord says, "Let my people go!" (*Sing.*)

Go Down, Moses

African American spiritual
arranged by Harry Thacker Burleigh

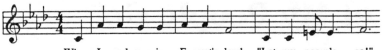

When Is-rael was in E-gypt's land, "Let my peo-ple go!"

Op-pressed so hard they could not stand, "Let my peo-ple go!"

Go down Mos-es, 'way down in E-gypt's land,——

Tell old Pha - raoh,—— "Let my peo-ple go!"

Egypt filled with frogs. Frogs were hopping and croaking everywhere. They finally bothered the pharaoh enough that he called in Moses. "Pray to your God," he said, "and ask that these frogs be taken away, and then I will let the people go." So Moses prayed, and the frogs died. But as soon as the frogs were gone, the pharaoh changed his mind and said the Hebrews couldn't leave after all. (*Continue to tell the story, briefly describing the plagues of gnats, flies, disease and death of livestock, animals, boils, hail, locusts, and darkness. Sing the last two lines of the song each time Moses tells Pharaoh, "The Lord says, 'Let my people go!'"*)

The pharaoh would still not let God's people go. He was stubborn and would not listen to Moses, even though God had sent plagues of blood, frogs, gnats, flies, death of animals, boils, hail, locusts, and darkness. God decided to try one last time to force the pharaoh to free the Hebrew slaves. God knew the only way the pharaoh would listen was if something really terrible happened to him and to the people of Egypt. So Moses went back to Pharaoh with one last message: "The Lord, God of Israel says that if you do not let the Hebrew people go, all the first-born sons of Egypt will die. Your oldest son will die, and every oldest boy in every family in Egypt will also die. The Lord says, 'Let my people go!' " (*Sing.*)

But the pharaoh still wouldn't listen. Now God didn't want any of the Hebrew boys to be killed, so the Lord gave Moses special instructions. The Hebrew people were told to cook lamb or goat meat for dinner on a particular night and then smear some of the animal's blood around the front door of their houses. They were then to pack up their things and get ready to travel.

The people did what Moses told them to do. They smeared the animal blood around their doors on the night they were supposed to. That night, the spirit of death spread over the land of Egypt. It killed the oldest son in each Egyptian family, including the pharaoh's. But the spirit of death 'passed over' the homes marked with blood on the doors, and none of the Hebrew boys died.

Finally, the pharaoh listened. He told Moses to take the Hebrews and get out of Egypt—*now*! He didn't want any more to do with them or their God. The people were packed and ready to go, and that night the Hebrews began their walk out of slavery to freedom in the promised land.

Let's Pray. Dear God, sometimes we don't listen to what is good for us, just like the pharaoh didn't listen to Moses. Help us to be less stubborn than he was. Amen.

TWELFTH SUNDAY AFTER PENTECOST   Proper 14
Exodus 14:19–31   Crossing the Red Sea

Finding the Way

Prop Needed
A road map of the United States, with the route from your town
to Disneyland or Disney World highlighted with marker

The Message
Have any of you ever taken a long trip in the car with your family? Maybe you drove to visit your grandparents who live in another state, or maybe you went on vacation someplace far away,
such as Disneyland or the beach or the mountains.

If we're going someplace close to home—say, to the grocery
store or a friend's house—we usually know the way, don't we? We
just go there without thinking about it. But if we're going someplace far away, we often use a map to help us.

Here is a may of the United States. (*Show the map.*) This map
shows the shape of each state and all the major highways you can
take to get from one place to another. Here's where we live. (*Point
to location on the map.*) Suppose we wanted to go from our town
to Disneyland (*or Disney World, if you live too close to Disneyland
to make the point.*) Disneyland is in Anaheim, California, way
over here. (*Point to it.*)

The grown-ups going on your vacation would study the map
and decide which roads would be the best ones to take to Disneyland. I marked the route I think is best with a highlight marker.
(*Point out route.*) I would keep this map with me in the front seat
of my car and check it often to make sure I was on the right high-
way to get to Disneyland.

At the end of our story last week, Moses was leading the Hebrews out of Egypt to the promised land. There was just one problem. None of the people knew how to get there, not even Moses!
They didn't have a map to help guide them either. But this time
they didn't need a map. God knew where the promised land was
and showed the people the way. During the day God appeared to
the people as a great tall cloud and at night as a tall pillar of fire.

The people followed the cloud and the fire as God led them toward their new home.

The Hebrews were gone from Egypt only a short time when the pharaoh changed his mind *again*. He felt sorry that he had let his slaves go, and decided to chase them and bring them back to Egypt. He took his army, his horses, and his war chariots. He would fight to get his slaves back if he had to.

The Hebrews were at the edge of a big body of water called the Red Sea when they saw the Egyptian army behind them. They were trapped—water in front of them, and their enemies behind them. What do you think the people did? Did they trust God, who had led them this far, to somehow rescue them from the Egyptians? No. They panicked. They whined and complained to Moses, "Why did you bring us out of Egypt, just to be killed in the desert?" But Moses told the people to hush, and they would see how powerful their God really was.

Then the Lord caused the wind to blow. It blew and blew. The water in the Red Sea divided. It split in half, and a path appeared where the water used to be. The people walked across the path, with great walls of water on either side of them, until they reached the other shore safely.

Pharaoh still would not give up. He ordered his army to chase the Hebrews on the path God had made. With their horses and chariots, the soldiers followed God's people. Once they were on the path, the great walls of water on both sides of them came crashing down, drowning all of the Egyptians. The Hebrews were safe at last. Finally, they knew how strong and powerful their God was. They had faith in the Lord and in Moses and were ready to travel through the desert to their new home.

Let's Pray. Dear God, thank you for being our God. May we grow in faith every day. Amen.

THIRTEENTH SUNDAY AFTER   Proper 15
PENTECOST   God's Gracious Gifts
Exodus 16:2–15

Manna from Heaven

Prop Needed

A picture of the desert in the Middle East

The Message

Good morning, boys and girls. Last week, we heard how Moses led the Hebrews out of Egypt and through the Red Sea. The pharaoh and his army tried to follow the Hebrews and take them back to Egypt, but the Egyptians drowned. The Hebrews were safe at last, and they headed toward the promised land with the Lord showing them the way.

It was a very long walk from Egypt to the promised land, so long that it would take the Hebrews forty years. And most of what they had to walk through was desert. Here is a picture of what the desert looked like. (*Show the picture.*) You can see that it was a very dry place, with lots of sand and very few plants.

The Hebrews were only out of Egypt a few days when they started to worry. "What are we going to eat out here in this dry, sandy desert?" they asked. They complained to Moses, "Why did you bring us out of Egypt anyway? Even though we were slaves, we at least had enough food to eat there."

The Lord said to Moses, "I am going to give food to my people. Every day it will rain down from the sky. They are to gather just enough food for that day, not any extra to save. Except on the sixth day, they should collect enough food for two days so they don't have to work on the Sabbath, the day of rest."

Moses told the people to come together in the morning. When everyone was there, the Lord appeared to them as a dazzling light in a cloud. God said to Moses, "I have heard the complaints of my people. Tell them that in the evening I will give them meat to eat. In the morning, they will have as much bread as they want. Then they will know that I, the Lord, am their God. Maybe then they will finally trust me to take care of them."

That evening, just before suppertime, a large flock of quails flew into the camp. Quails are small birds which are very good to eat. In the morning, dew covered the ground. Have you ever gone outside early in the morning, and the grass is all wet, but it hasn't rained the night before? That wet moisture in the grass is called dew. But the dew the Hebrews found was special. When it dried, there was something thin and flaky—kind of like small white seeds—left on the desert ground.

The people asked, "What is this stuff?" And Moses told them that it was the food God had promised them. It was called 'manna.' Can you say that? Manna. Good! Moses told the people how much to collect. Most of the people listened and only took what they needed for that day. Some, however, still didn't trust God. They were afraid there might not be any manna the next day, so they took extra and hid it. But when they checked their hidden manna the following morning, it was rotten and full of worms! And when they looked outside their tents, there was fresh manna on the ground.

God was disappointed in those who had failed to trust in God's goodness. Even so, the Lord gave the people the gift of food every day for the forty years they were in the desert wilderness.

It is still God who gives us the gift of food today. What is your favorite thing to eat? (*Pause for answers.*) All good things to eat are God's gifts to us. God provides the sunshine, the rain, and the rich soil that plants need to grow and the things animals need to be strong. God gives the farmers and ranchers the intelligence to figure out the best way to grow crops and raise livestock.

All the good things in our lives are gifts from God. Our family, our friends, our homes, our schools, even our food—all of them come to us because God loves us and wants to take care of us.

You would think that after all that God did for them, the Hebrews would learn to trust the Lord and not complain every time something went wrong, wouldn't you? It seems that they were slow learners though, because they still crabbed about many things before they reached the promised land. We'll hear more about that next week.

Let's Pray. Dear God, we thank you for the many, many gifts you have given us. Help us to be grateful. Help us trust you to take care of us, rather than complaining every time something goes wrong. Amen.

God the Thirst-Quencher

Prop Needed
A glass of water

The Message
Have you ever been really, really thirsty? Maybe you were playing hard outside on a hot summer day, and all of a sudden you realized how thirsty you were. You probably went inside your house and poured yourself a glass of water to drink. (*Hold up glass.*) Or, if you were at a playground, you probably got a drink from a drinking fountain, didn't you?

Have you ever been really, really thirsty in a place where there was nothing to drink—maybe on a long ride in the car, or on a hike when your canteen is empty? That can be hard, can't it? All you can think about is a glass of cool water or some yummy juice, and there isn't any. But you know if you wait a little while, your mom or dad will stop the car at a gas station, or you'll be home, or the hike will be finished, and you'll be able to get a drink and feel much better.

The Hebrews were traveling from place to place in the desert. The Lord would lead them to one spot where they'd set up camp and stay for awhile. Then it would be time to move on to another place, where they'd set up camp again. Every morning the Lord provided manna for the people to eat, and every evening, quail.

One place the Hebrews were led to was called Rephidim. The Lord told them to set up camp, but there was no water. The desert can be a very dangerous place, especially if there is no water. People need water to live. They need even more water in the desert, because the sun is so hot and the air is so dry. In the desert, human beings would die in just a few days without water.

When the Hebrews saw that they were going to camp in a place with no water, they were afraid. Do you know what they did? Did they pray to the Lord who had brought them this far, to please give them some water to drink? No. They complained to Moses again. They not only complained about being thirsty, but they also complained about being brought out of slavery in Egypt. "Why did you bring us out of Egypt? So you could kill us all with thirst in the desert?" Once again, the people failed to have faith and trust in the Lord.

Moses prayed and asked God what he should do. God told Moses to take some of the Hebrew leaders and a special walking stick he had and go to a rock at Mount Sinai. "Hit the rock with the stick," said the Lord, "and clean water will come out for the people to drink." Moses hit the rock with his stick, and the Hebrew leaders watched with surprise as clear, clean water streamed out of the rock.

The Hebrews named the place where this happened 'Masseh' and 'Meribah,' which means 'testing' and 'complaining,' because the people had complained to Moses and tested God by asking, "Is God with us or not?"

I think the most amazing thing about this story is not water coming out of a rock, although that is pretty fantastic. The most amazing thing about the story is how much God loved the people. Over and over again, the Hebrews failed to have faith and trust in God. All they ever seemed to do was complain. They complained when the pharaoh's army was closing in on them at the Red Sea, they cried for food, and they cried for water. Even though they complained over and over again instead of trusting God, God continued to take care of them.

This is called 'grace.' When God takes care of us even if we don't deserve it, it's called grace. God's grace is not given to us because we're good all the time. No one can be good *all* the time. We all make mistakes and sometimes do naughty things or fail in one way or another. But God still takes care of us, gives us grace, because God loves us. God's love is great enough to forgive us when we fail.

Let's Pray. Thank you God, for your amazing grace. Thank you for the stories in the Bible that tell us how you helped your people long ago, and thank you for taking good care of us today. In Jesus' name. Amen.

To Be or Not To Be

Props Needed
A bowl of bite-sized pretzels
A bowl of bite-sized peanut-butter crackers

The Message
Are you good at making decisions? If you have to make a choice between two things, do you usually take a long time, or do you decide pretty quickly? Are you usually happy with your decision once you've made it?

I have two bowls with snacks in them. One bowl has pretzels, and the other has peanut butter crackers. You may each have a snack, but only one. You have to choose between a pretzel or a peanut butter cracker. (*Pass around the bowls, and allow each child to make his or her choice.*) Did everybody get one? Is everybody happy with the snack they chose? Okay, go ahead and eat.

Some decisions are a lot harder than others, aren't they? What are some of the hard choices you've had to make? (*Listen to answers.*) In our story today, God gives the Hebrews an important choice to make.

The people left Rephidim, where God gave them water from the rock. Then God led them to the base, or foot, of a tall mountain called Mount Sinai. Mount Sinai was God's special mountain. It is where Moses first met God at the burning bush.

The people camped at the bottom of Mount Sinai, and Moses went up the mountain to talk to God. The Lord told Moses to tell the people. "You saw how I saved you from the Egyptians. Like a mother eagle carries her babies on her wings, I brought you here to me, on this holy mountain. Now, if you will obey me and the laws I give you, then you will be my chosen people."

God was giving the Hebrew people a choice. Did they want to continue to be God's people or not? God had made a promise to Abraham, that Abraham and his descendants would always be God's people, and the Lord would always be their God. The promise had been passed down from Abraham and Sarah, to Isaac and Rebecca, to Jacob and Rachel. Now it was the Hebrews' turn to decide for themselves whether or not they would accept the promise given to their ancestors and still be God's people. Were they willing to obey God and be the chosen people, or did they want to give up God's promise and try to make it on their own?

Moses called the Hebrew leaders together and told them what God had said. All the people answered together, "Yes, we want to be your people, God! All that you have spoken, we will do." The Hebrews wanted to be God's people still. They promised to obey God, and God promised that they would still be the chosen people.

God made a promise to the people, and the people made a promise to God. Another word for promise is *covenant*. Can you say that? Covenant. A covenant is a very serious promise made between two people, two groups of people, a person and God, or a group of people and God. Those who choose to make this kind of serious promise are in a covenant relationship together. People who marry one another are in a covenant relationship. Their promise, or covenant, as well as their love, binds them together. The Hebrews decided that they wanted to continue being in a covenant relationship with God.

God offers us the same choice offered to the Hebrews. We can decide whether we want to be God's people or try to make it on our own. We can decide to be in a covenant relationship with God or not. When we choose to love and worship God, to come to church to learn more about God, to love and care about others, then we are choosing God's promise. All of us are here because we want to be in a covenant relationship with God. Just as the Hebrews said yes to the choice God gave them, we also say yes to God.

Let's Pray. Dear God, thank you for offering us the choice to join you in a covenant relationship. Thank you for your love and care. Amen.

The Face of God

Props Needed
A large piece of drawing paper on an easel
Colored markers, pencils, or some other drawing medium
An artistic assistant

The Message
(*Set up the storytelling space with your assistant standing at the easel. The easel should be positioned so that the children cannot see the picture as it is being drawn.*)

Do you ever wonder what God looks like? If you were to draw a picture of God, what would you draw? (*As children describe God's appearance, have the assistant draw the description to the best of her or his ability. Children might need prompting, such as: "Does God have a face? What do you think God's face looks like?" If children have ideas, turn the picture around when they are finished and ask, "Is this what you think God looks like?" If, from the beginning, children say we cannot draw God because no one has ever seen God, because God is a spirit who doesn't have a body, or for some other reason, turn the blank paper around and agree with them. Say something like, "You're right. No one knows what God looks like, so how can we draw a picture of God? Pick up story where appropriate.*)

Actually no one has ever seen God so no one really knows what God looks like. In the Bible, people saw God in many different ways. Moses met God in the burning bush. The Hebrews followed the Lord, who looked like a pillar of cloud and a pillar of fire. When Jesus was baptized, God came down from heaven looking like a dove. The dove rested on Jesus' shoulder and said, "You are my beloved child, and I am very happy with you." But God doesn't always look like a bush, a cloud, a fire, or a dove. The Lord chooses to look like these things at special times to help people understand God better.

People think about God in different ways, too. This also helps them to understand the Lord better. Jesus called God 'father,' and many people think of God as a loving father. The prayer that Jesus taught his disciples begins: "Our Father, who art in heaven." The Bible also refers to God as a mother—a mother eagle who carries her young on her wings (Exodus 19:4) and a mother who comforts her children (Isaiah 66:13). But just because we sometimes think of God as a father or a mother does not mean that God is a man or a woman. It means that God loves us, protects us, and cares for us just as good parents care for their children.

God is a spirit. The Lord doesn't have a body like you and I have. God is invisible, like the wind. We can't see the wind, but we know it's there. We can feel it against our skin, and we can see what the wind does. Sometimes it causes ripples across the water of a lake, or it causes trees to bend. God is like the wind. We can't see God, but we can feel God's presence with us. We can see what the Lord does by looking at all the good in the world.

In last week's story, the Hebrews decided that yes, they wanted to be God's people, and they would do whatever the Lord told them to do. A very important meeting was to take place on Mount Sinai between God and Moses. The people knew that God was there, even though they were not allowed to see the Lord. God sent thunder and lightning, a thick cloud covered the mountain, and the people heard a loud trumpet blast. Next, the Lord sent fire, and thick smoke covered the mountain. I imagine it may have looked like a smoking volcano. Meanwhile, the trumpet sound grew louder and louder.

The Lord told Moses not to let the people onto the mountain. They were supposed to stay at the bottom so they could not see God. But the people didn't need to see the Lord to know that God was there. They could feel God's presence and see God's power at work on the mountain. Then Moses climbed Mount Sinai to speak with the Lord. Next week, we'll find out what this special meeting was about.

Let's Pray. Almighty Lord, we may not be able to see you, but we know you are with us and that you love us. We love you too, God, and thank you for all your blessings. Amen.

SEVENTEENTH SUNDAY AFTER   Proper 19
PENTECOST   The Ten Commandments
Exodus 20:1–20

It's Cool to Follow the Rules

Props Needed
None

The Message

Today we're going to talk about rules. What is a rule? (*Pause for answers.*) Right. It's something you're supposed to follow. A rule is something that helps us know how we're supposed to behave, isn't it?

Do you have rules in your family? What are some of your family's rules? (*Pause for answers. If children have problems thinking of family rules help them get started by sharing one of yours.*) What about school? Are there rules at school? What are some of those rules? (*Listen and repeat children's answers.*)

There are rules in families, schools, clubs, cities, countries, even churches. Wherever people live or work or play together, there are rules. Why do we have rules? (*Pause for answers.*) Some rules help keep us safe, rules such as 'Don't cross the street by yourself,' and 'Don't talk to strangers.' Other rules are to make sure we don't hurt other people and other people don't hurt us, rules such as 'No hitting,' and 'Don't throw rocks.' Rules are important because they help us get along with one another, and they help keep us safe. There was a commercial on TV a couple of years ago that had a group of kids talking about rules and how important they are. The commercial ended with one child saying, "It's cool to follow the rules." And it *is* cool to follow the rules. What would happen if everyone decided that they weren't going to follow rules anymore? If each person did whatever he or she wanted? It would be a mess, wouldn't it? You couldn't ride in a car because you would have no idea what the other drivers were going to do. It wouldn't be safe to play on the playground, because someone might shove you off a swing when he didn't want to wait his turn. Or you might get hit by a flying rock someone just felt like throwing. We all need rules to help guide us, and it's cool to follow rules.

God's people needed some rules too, and that was what the big meeting on Mount Sinai between God and Moses was all about. Remember God had asked the Hebrews if they still wanted to be the chosen people, and they said yes. So the Lord met with Moses and said, "Tell the Hebrews that because they are my people, and I am their God, here is how they are to treat me and one another. . . . Here are the rules."

Then God gave Moses the Ten Commandments. They are:
1. Worship no other gods but the Lord.
2. Do not worship idols. In other words, nothing was supposed to be more important to the people than God.
3. Do not swear or use God's name disrespectfully.
4. Rest on the Sabbath. The people were supposed to work only six days a week and worship God and rest on the seventh day, Saturday.
5. Respect your father and mother.
6. Do not murder anyone.
7. Do not commit adultery. This means that people who are married are supposed to love each other in a special way.
8. Do not steal.
9. Do not lie.
10. Do not covet. This means that if your friend has something, you are supposed to be happy for her rather than wanting the thing for your own.

God gave the Hebrews these ten rules to help them live as the people of God. The commandments taught the people how to treat their Lord and one another with respect and love. We are the people of God today. These ten rules, commandments, can help us learn how to treat God and one another with love and respect as well.

Jesus summed up these ten commandments in just two simple rules: One, love the Lord your God with all your heart, all your strength, and all your mind; and two, love your neighbor as yourself. Either way—with ten rules or two—it's cool to follow the rules.

Let's Pray. Dear God, we thank you for giving us the Ten Commandments to help us live the way you want us to. In Jesus' name. Amen.

A Second Chance

Props Needed
Flannel board
Flannel-board figures (found in the Appendix)

The Message
Who can remember where our story left off last week? (*Pause for answers.*) Moses met God on Mount Sinai, and God gave him the Ten Commandments. Before going up the mountain, Moses left his brother and helper, Aaron, in charge of the people.

Moses was on Mount Sinai quite a long time, and the Hebrews began to wonder what had happened to him. Then they began to worry. Finally they became afraid. They were afraid something awful had happened and that Moses wouldn't come back. They felt left and all alone, and they complained to Aaron. (*Follow the story with flannel-board figures.*)

"We don't know what's happened to Moses, the one who led us out of Egypt. So make us a god to lead us from now on."

The Hebrews lived thousands of years ago. In those days most people believed that there were lots of gods, not just one. The thing that made the Hebrews special was that they worshipped only one God—Yahweh. It was Yahweh who freed them from slavery in Egypt and was leading them to the promised land. Yahweh was their God, and they were Yahweh's people. That was the covenant—or promise—God had offered them, and they had agreed to it, remember? But now they felt unsure of everything because Moses was taking so long. So, instead of being patient and faithful while they waited, they asked Aaron to make them a new god to worship.

Aaron told them to give him all of their gold jewelry. He put the jewelry in a big pot over a fire and heated it until it melted. Then he poured the melted gold into a mold. When the hot metal cooled and hardened, Aaron took off the mold, and there stood a shining golden calf. When the people saw the golden calf, they were very pleased. They shouted, "Here is our god, who led us out of Egypt."

Then Aaron built an altar so everyone could worship the calf. He announced, "Tomorrow there will be a festival to honor our new god." The next day, the Hebrews threw a party like no one had ever seen before—a party to honor their new god, the golden calf.

Meanwhile, Yahweh and Moses were still talking up on Mount Sinai. Moses didn't know what the people were up to at the bottom of the mountain, but Yahweh sure did. How do you think the Lord felt when the people called a statue made of gold their god and gave it the credit for bringing them out of Egypt? (*Pause for answers.*) Yes, I'll bet the Lord felt hurt and angry, don't you think?

The Lord told Moses he'd better get back down the mountain. "Your people have already sinned and rejected me," Yahweh said. "Don't try to stop me. I am angry with them and am going to destroy them all."

But Moses begged the Lord to think about it some more. He reminded God of the promise made with Abraham and the people to always be their god and give them a land of their own. So the Lord decided that he would not destroy all the people after all but would give them a second chance.

Moses then went down the mountain to see just how bad things were. He carried with him the two stone tablets on which the Lord had written the Ten Commandments. When he got to the bottom of the mountain, Moses could not believe his eyes. He saw the people of God praising and dancing around a silly gold statue shaped like a calf. They were acting like fools. Moses became so angry that he threw down the stone tablets, and they smashed into a million pieces.

Moses melted the golden calf and ground it up into a powdery dust. Then he mixed it with water and made the people drink it so that they would realize there was nothing special about the statue they were worshipping. It was just a fake god, what we call an 'idol.'

The people were punished for their sin, but God did give them another chance. After all, they were God's people, and even with all the mistakes they had made, Yahweh still loved them.

Let's Pray. Dear Yahweh God, we know that we sometimes make mistakes, too. Thank you for giving us second chances and for loving us even when we do something wrong. In Jesus' name. Amen.

How Do You Feel?

Props and Preparation Needed
From magazines cut faces of people, preferably children, expressing various emotions, including anger. Mount the pictures on construction paper or recycled file folders.

The Message
Good morning, boys and girls. How are you feeling this morning? Good? Well, I'm glad. I have with me some pictures. I will hold up each picture so you can see it, and you tell me how you think the person in the photo is feeling.

Here's the first one. How do you think the little girl in this picture is feeling? (*Hold up the pictures, one at a time. Allow the children to respond to each. If there is a difference of opinion on any given photo, acknowledge that it is okay to disagree. There are no right or wrong answers. Save the picture of the angry person for last.*) What about this person? How does he feel? (*Pause.*) Angry? How do you know he is angry? (*Pause.*)

Do you ever get angry? (*Pause.*) What things make you really mad? (*Pause.*) What do you feel like doing when you're angry? Let's say a toy won't work the way you want it to—what do you want to do then? Suppose your brother or sister is picking on you and making you mad. Maybe he or she is calling you names or messing up a project you're trying to work on—what do you feel like doing to show him or her how angry you are? Or maybe you're watching TV or playing Nintendo, and your mom or dad tells you to stop what you're doing and clean your room. Or maybe one of them yells at you for something you didn't do, without giving you a chance to explain. What do you want to do in a case like that? (*Some of your examples should come from those given earlier by the children themselves. Give opportunities for responses throughout the conversation.*)

It's okay to be angry. Everyone gets angry sometimes. Even people who love each other very much—like parents and kids or brothers and sisters—sometimes get mad at each other. Even God gets mad now and then. Remember how angry God was at the Hebrews when they built and worshipped the golden calf? So mad that God wanted to kill all the people then and there. But Moses talked God into giving the people another chance.

Next the Lord decided to send the people on toward the promised land with an angel as their guide instead of God. God was afraid of getting that angry at the people again. Once more, however, Moses stepped in and reminded the Lord of the promise to always be with the Hebrew people. So, once again, God's mind was changed by Moses, and the Lord went with the people, guiding them toward the promised land.

It's okay to be angry, but sometimes what we do with our anger is not okay. (*Again, take examples from the suggestions given by the children, where appropriate.*) Throwing toys does not make them cooperate any better and can be dangerous. Your toy might get broken, or someone might get hurt. Hitting, kicking, biting, or pushing are not okay, either. Again, someone might get hurt. Hurting others, even when we're angry, is not okay. Shouting back at our parents usually doesn't do us any good, either. It just gets us into more trouble.

There *are* acceptable ways to show anger, though. If your toy won't cooperate, you might walk away from it and play with something else for a while, then go back later to the thing that gave you trouble. Next time you're really, really mad at someone, you might try pounding your pillow as hard as you can with your fists instead of pounding on your brother or sister. You could go outside and kick a ball with all your might, or throw a soft foam ball inside the house. You could ask your mom for some scratch paper and tear it to shreds. Or use the paper to draw a picture about how you feel. What colors would you use if you were to draw a picture about being angry? (*Pause.*) You could go into your room, shut the door, and bang out some loud music on your xylophone or another musical instrument.

There are many things we can do to let out our anger, things that won't hurt other people or ourselves. One of the best things we can do is talk to the people we're mad at, either when we're angry or after we've calmed down. You can say something like, "It really makes me angry when you call me names," or "I feel really mad when you do that, Mom." When we talk with others about our feelings, it helps us understand and get along with each other better.

Finally, we can always pray to God to help us handle our feelings—whether we're angry, sad, or frightened. God likes it when we share our feelings in prayer, good feelings and those feelings that sometimes scare us such as anger. Sharing our feelings with God and others in positive ways can be very helpful.

Let's Pray. Dear God, we thank you for the many feelings you give us. Help us learn to deal with all of our emotions in positive ways. Amen.

The Best One
for the Job

Prop Needed
The ordained officers of your congregation

The Message
For several weeks we've been talking about Moses, the Hebrews, and the search for the land God had promised. Moses worked for God, leading the people where the Lord directed and acting as a messenger between God and the people. It was a tough job, but Moses did it well, and the people were guided through the barren desert for forty years. Forty years is a long time, isn't it? For forty years Moses was the leader of God's people.

Finally Moses was getting old. He knew that he would die soon and didn't want to leave the Hebrews alone in the desert without a leader. So he asked God to choose someone to take his place, someone to be the new leader of God's people.

The Lord chose a man named Joshua to take over the job for Moses. Joshua was chosen because God knew he would be able to handle the job. We don't know if he was the kindest or the wisest or even the most faithful person in the community, but he was the best person for this particular job. God gave Joshua the skills he would need to lead the people into the promised land and begin their lives in their new home. So Joshua took over as leader from Moses.

There was a special ceremony to let the people know who their new leader was. Everyone gathered together to participate in the ceremony. Joshua stood in front of Eleazar, who was the minister or priest of the people. Then Moses put his hands on Joshua's head and told everybody that Joshua was their new leader and that they should follow him.

We have people in our church who serve as leaders of the congregation. They are chosen because, like Joshua, they have special skills that make them good at certain jobs. Each year, the people in the church decide who they want as their leaders. An election is held, and the congregation votes to decide who the leaders will be. (*Adapt this section to reflect your own denomination's polity and the circumstances of your particular church.*)

One group of leaders is called the deacons. The deacons work mostly with older people, people who are sick, and the poor. The deacons take the flowers that are in church each Sunday to people in the hospital. They visit members of our congregation who are sick and unable to come to church. They also collect food for people who don't have enough to eat and come to our church asking for help. People who are chosen as deacons should be loving, caring people who like to share themselves with others. Would all the members of the congregation who are ordained deacons please stand up? These are the deacons of our church.

Another group of leaders in our church is called elders. The elders are responsible for running the church. They make sure we have church school for children and adults, that we have worship every Sunday, and that we share with others through mission programs. The elders are also responsible for keeping the church building in good working order, for handling all the church's money, and for dealing with problems that come up. People chosen as elders need to be dedicated, hard-working, and organized. They should also have good ideas and know how to get things done. Will all of the elders of the congregation please stand up? These are the elders of our church.

The last leaders of the church are the pastors. The pastors' job is to be the spiritual leader of the congregation. The pastors preach sermons, visit the sick and lonely, help people with their problems, lead Bible studies, pray for people, and do many other things that help us to understand God better and love God more. Will our pastors, the Reverend _____ and the Reverend _____, please stand?

All of these church leaders—deacons, elders, and pastors—are chosen because we believe they will do their jobs well. When people become deacons, elders, or pastors, a special service is held called an ordination. All the people of the church gather together in worship. The new leaders kneel down in the front of the church. Then all those who are already deacons, elders, or pastors lay their hands on the heads and shoulders of the new leaders being ordained. The pastor says a prayer, asking God to bless the work of these dedicated people, then everyone shakes hands, and the work of ministry continues.

Let's Pray. Dear God, thank you for giving each of us our own special talents and skills. Help all of us to listen to the leaders you have given us. Amen.

TWENTY-FIRST SUNDAY AFTER   Proper 23
PENTECOST   Review of Moses' Cycle
Deuteronomy 34:1–12

Moses Revisited

Props Needed
Flannel board
Flannel-board figures (found in the Appendix)

The Message
Today we come to the end of the long story about Moses. Let's
go over some of the things we've learned about Moses.

He was born a Hebrew in a country called Egypt. At that time,
the king of Egypt, the pharaoh, was killing all the Hebrew baby
boys, so what did his mother do to save him? (*Pause for answers.*)
She put him into a basket on the river Nile and hoped someone
would rescue him. (*Put picture of Moses in basket on flannel
board.*) The pharaoh's daughter found Moses, and he grew up in
the palace.

When Moses was a young man, he was forced to run away from
Egypt. Do you remember why? (*Pause for answers.*) Moses' people,
the Hebrews, were slaves in Egypt. One day, when Moses saw an
Egyptian murder a Hebrew slave, he became very angry and
killed the Egyptian himself. (*Put up picture of Moses killing
Egyptian.*) Moses had to run away or the king would have killed
him. He went to a country called Midian. There he married, had
children, and worked for his father-in-law.

One day while Moses was taking care of some sheep, he saw
something very strange. Do you remember what it was? It was a
bush that looked like it was on fire, but it was not burning up.
(*Put up picture of the burning bush.*)

God spoke to Moses from the burning bush and told him there
was a very important job for him to do. What was that job?
(*Pause.*) God wanted Moses to go back to Egypt, tell the pharaoh
to free the Hebrew slaves, and then take the Hebrews to the land
God had promised Abraham.

Moses didn't really want to do it, but he obeyed God and returned to Egypt. It took a very long time and many awful
plagues—plagues of blood in the river, frogs, gnats, flies, disease,
boils, hail, locusts, darkness, and finally death of the first-born

sons of the Egyptians—to convince the pharaoh to let God's people go. Finally, after his own son died, the pharaoh agreed to free the slaves.

The Hebrews left Egypt and headed toward the promised land. But when they got to the Red Sea, who did they see chasing them? (*Pause.*) That's right. The pharaoh and his army. So God split the sea, leaving a path in the middle where the water used to be. Moses directed the people to walk on the path, and they arrived safely on the other side. (*Put up picture of parting of the Red Sea.*) When the Egyptians tried to follow, the water returned, and they were drowned.

Moses led the people through the desert for a long, long time—forty years. Were the people happy travelers? (*Pause.*) No, they complained a lot, didn't they? But Moses never gave up on them, and neither did God. Moses led his people on the journey to the promised land and also led them in their faith journey. He tried to help them understand that God was faithful and could be trusted to care for them.

One very important thing that happened while the Hebrews were in the desert took place on Mount Sinai. It was there that God gave Moses the Ten Commandments, the rules that the people of God were expected to follow. (*Put up the picture of stone tablets with Ten Commandments on them.*)

At last, the people were near the land God had promised. Although Moses led the people for forty years, he never made it to the promised land himself. He went up a high mountain, and from there he could see the land that would be the Hebrews' new home, but he died just before getting there. The Bible tells us that Moses was not allowed to enter the promised land because one time in the desert when he had followed God's instructions and provided water for the people out of a rock, he took the credit himself instead of giving it to God.

Even so, with the Lord guiding him, Moses did a great job. He brought the people out of slavery and led them through the barren desert to their new home. When Moses died, Joshua took his place as leader of the Hebrews. The people entered the promised land and built farms and cities and a great nation, just as God had promised. The country they built was called Israel. Israel has never had a leader as great or as faithful to God as Moses.

Let's Pray. Dear God, we thank you for great people of faith like Moses. Help us to learn from their stories how we can be faithful too. Amen.

TWENTY-SECOND SUNDAY AFTER   Proper 24
PENTECOST   Universality of the Gospel
Ruth 1:1–19a; Psalm 146;
1 Thessalonians 1:1–10

Being Chosen

Preparation Needed
Be familiar with the nursery game, "The Farmer in the Dell"

The Message
Who has played the game, "The Farmer in the Dell"? (*If some
haven't played it, explain the game.*) Everyone stands in a circle,
holding hands. The person who is chosen as the farmer stands in
the middle of the circle. Then everyone sings the first verse of the
song, which goes like this:

> The farmer in the dell,
> The farmer in the dell,
> Hi-ho the derry-o,
> The farmer in the dell.

Then everyone sings the second verse.

> The farmer takes a wife,
> The farmer takes a wife,
> Hi-ho the derry-o,
> The farmer takes a wife.

While the group is singing the second verse, the farmer chooses
a person from the circle to stand with him in the center and be
his wife. During each verse, the last chosen person picks someone
to stand in the center and be the child, nurse, dog, cat, rat,
cheese, and so on until finally the cheese stands alone. Let's try
it, okay? Everyone hold hands in a circle. Johnny, would you like
to be the farmer? Okay, everybody. Sing. The farmer in the
dell . . . (*Play the game. If you do not have enough children to play
the complete game, you might want to choose volunteers from the*

congregation or ask the youth to join you at the beginning of the story. Also, if you have a nursery tape or record with the song on it, you might want to use that to help lead the singing.)

Very good! That was fun, wasn't it? "The Farmer in the Dell" is a game that involves choosing people, isn't it? People are chosen to be the farmer, the wife, the child, and so on. There are lots of other times in life when people are chosen for something. Can you think of a time when you were chosen for something? *(Pause for answers. If they have trouble coming up with examples, help get them started with some of your own.)* Have you ever been chosen to be on a ball team? Or in a play? Maybe you were chosen to sing a solo in choir, or read the Bible story in Sunday school. Or perhaps your mom chose you to take out the garbage!

Sometimes we're chosen to do a thing because we're especially good at doing what needs to be done, such as playing first base, or singing. We deserve to be chosen because we've earned it. Other times we're chosen because we're the only person who happens to be around at the time, such as being chosen to take out the garbage. How do you feel if you really want to do something, and you're *not* chosen? *(Pause.)* That can feel pretty crummy, can't it?

We've talked a lot during the past few months about God's chosen people, the Hebrews. God chose the Hebrews to be in a special relationship. Yahweh would always be their God, and the Hebrews would always be Yahweh's people. God made this promise with the chosen people thousands of years ago.

A long time later, Jesus was born. Jesus' family lived in Israel and were Hebrews. They were a part of God's chosen people, but when Jesus grew up and started to preach, he had an unusual message for God's people to hear. God's promise was for *all* people. You did not have to be a Hebrew to be of the chosen people. God loves everyone and chooses all of us to be a part of God's family. God doesn't choose us only after we've proven that we're good enough to be chosen. God chooses us right now, just the way we are . . . not because we deserve it, but because God loves us. God's family is big enough to include everyone who wants to be in it. It's not like a baseball team that can use only nine players or an orchestra that needs only ten violins. God's family can hold as many people as want to join.

God loves all people and wants them to understand and know God as their Lord and their friend. It doesn't matter what color your skin is, what country you're from, or how rich you are—God loves you and wants you to be part of the chosen people, the family of God.

You and I are part of God's chosen people. We come together each Sunday as a family to worship, to learn, and to help one another, as do people in churches around the world. The promises God made to Abraham are promises made to us as well. Yahweh will always be our God, and we will always be Yahweh's people.

Let's Pray. Dear God, we thank you for choosing to love and care for us and all people. Help us to share your love with others. Amen.

Love Is the Strongest Medicine

Props Needed

A stethoscope, tongue depressor, or another easily recognizable piece of doctor's equipment

The Message

Who can tell me what I have with me this morning? (*Hold up prop and listen to answers.*) It's a stethoscope, isn't it? Who uses a stethoscope? (*Pause.*) Right. A doctor. And what does a doctor do with a stethoscope? (*Pause.*) How many of you have ever been to the doctor? Sometimes we go to the doctor because we're sick, don't we? And sometimes we go when we're healthy, for a checkup. Can you imagine what it would be like to be really, really sick and have no doctor to go to? If there were no doctors, we would be sick a lot more often and a lot longer each time. Without doctors and medicine to help make them well, many people would die. Even the shots we sometimes get at the doctor's office are very important because they keep us from getting very serious diseases. Doctors can't always make sick people well, but they can help most people. Our story this morning is about a man who became a very special doctor to some very special people. The doctor's name was Albert Schweitzer.

Albert Schweitzer was born in a country called Germany in 1875. His father was a Lutheran minister. Schweitzer was a brilliant man, a very good thinker. He liked to study and to write, and he wrote many books on different subjects. The first subject he wrote about was philosophy. A philosopher is someone who likes to think about life. Albert Schweitzer also studied and wrote about religion. His ideas were new, and not everyone agreed with what he said, but most people did agree that Albert Schweitzer was very smart.

He became a teacher at a university—or college—in Strassburg, Germany, and the pastor of a church. Schweitzer also played the organ very well. He studied the music of one particular composer, Johann Sebastian Bach, and wrote books about Bach and his music.

Albert Schweitzer had a bright future ahead of him. He could have been a world-famous teacher, or an author, or a concert organist. So his family and friends were naturally shocked when at the age of thirty-two he announced that he was going to study medicine and that he wanted to be a doctor in Africa.

He went to school for six years to become a doctor of medicine, and he married another doctor named Helene Bresslau. Together, the two went to deepest Africa, built a hospital clinic, and worked there for almost fifty years.

Life in Africa was not very comfortable. It was hot and humid, and there were wild animals and lots of bugs to contend with. The doctors at Schweitzer's hospital treated diseases that were uncommon in other parts of the world but very common in Africa—diseases such as sleeping sickness, leprosy, and malaria.

Dr. Schweitzer raised money for his hospital by giving organ concerts in Europe and by donating the money he earned from his books. He built the buildings with his own hands and with help from the native people.

But Helene and Albert Schweitzer's work paid off. As news of their hospital spread, Africans from as far away as five hundred miles came for help. They were poor people who couldn't pay for their treatment, but no one was turned away. The Schweitzers' work became known throughout the world. Doctors and nurses came from all over the globe to help heal people in the Schweitzers' hospital. In 1952, Albert Schweitzer won the Nobel Peace Prize for all the good, unselfish work he had done in Africa.

We might wonder why Albert Schweitzer would give up the comfortable life he had in Strassburg. He could have been a respected teacher, writer, or concert organist. Why did he throw all that away to go to a hot and buggy continent to practice medicine? He didn't know how things would turn out when he went to Africa. He didn't know that his clinic would become known throughout the world and that he would win the Nobel Peace Prize. Maybe the natives wouldn't trust him and wouldn't come to him for help. Or maybe he would get killed by a wild animal or die from one of the tropical diseases he was trying to treat. He took a big risk by giving up all he had worked for in Germany to become a doctor in Africa.

The reason Albert Schweitzer made that choice was because he loved God, and he loved people so much that he wanted to do all he could to serve them. Schweitzer felt that he could not be happy living a comfortable life in Europe when he knew that people in Africa were suffering and dying with no doctors to help them. So he decided to become a doctor himself, go to Africa, and do what he could to help heal the people there.

The best way we can show our love to God is by loving and helping other people. Albert and Helene Schweitzer are examples of two people who chose to do this with their lives. We don't all have to become doctors and work in Africa to show our love, however. You can start right here, right now, by being kind to those you meet, sharing with your brothers and sisters and friends, and doing helpful things for your parents and neighbors. Every time we do something unselfish for someone else, we are saying to God, "We love you."

Let's Pray. Dear God, we do love you, and we want you to know how much. Help us to show our love by loving others. Amen.

TWENTY-FOURTH SUNDAY AFTER   Proper 26
PENTECOST   Unselfish Giving
Matthew 23:1–12

Hillary and Mr. Morgan

Prop Needed
A metal tin filled with homemade cookies

The Message
Hillary Miller's father was transferred to a new office in a new town for his job. So the whole family—Hillary, her mom and dad, and their dog Max—moved to Springfield in the middle of July. Hillary would start the third grade in September. She was the new kid on the block.

When the moving van pulled up to their new house, lots of kids gathered on the sidewalk to watch. There were children on bikes and roller skates—big kids, little kids, and in-between kids. Hillary stood next to her mother on the front porch, and the movers rolled open the big, heavy doors on their truck. All of a sudden, the grown-ups were all very busy.

As the movers started bringing furniture and boxes into the house, Mr. and Mrs. Miller told them where to put what. Hillary stood on the lawn, trying to stay out of the way. A little girl with brown, curly hair walked slowly up to Hillary.

"Hi! My name's Valerie. What's yours?" the little girl said.

"Hillary," said Hillary.

"I live across the street in that yellow house with the green shutters. I have two brothers and a dog named Peanut. How about you?" Valerie asked.

"I have a dog named Max," said Hillary, "but no brothers or sisters."

"Max is a nice name. But you'd better make sure that Max stays out of old Mr. Morgan's garden. He's the grumpy man who lives next door to you. He doesn't like dogs or kids, especially if they're in his yard."

Hillary looked at Mr. Morgan's white house with the picket fence all around. "His yard sure looks neat and clean," she said. "Valerie, would you like to play with me in my new back yard? The people who used to live here left a swingset."

"I know," said Valerie. "Amy was my best friend. Sure, let's go."

Hillary and Valerie played together that afternoon and every day that week. They became good friends. They played on the swings at Hillary's house and went swimming in Valerie's pool. They played dolls together and walked their dogs together. Even Max and Peanut became friends.

Sometimes the girls saw Mr. Morgan working in his garden while they were swinging. He had pretty flowers, stickery rosebushes, and several apple trees in his yard. One time, the girls stood at the fence. "Hello!" they called to Mr. Morgan as he wrestled with an especially stubborn weed. He managed to grunt out a 'hello,' but kept right on working. Hillary and Valerie went back to the swingset.

The next day, it was too hot to swing. It was too hot to play dolls or even walk the dogs, so Hillary and Valerie went swimming. They played a long time in the pool, and at three o'clock they got out and dried themselves with towels. Valerie's mom brought them each a cool glass of lemonade, and they sat at the picnic table to drink it. Peanut was sitting on the grass, watching them, with his tongue hanging out.

"Look at poor Peanut," said Valerie. "He looks so hot."

"Yeah," said Hillary. "And he can't swim in the pool or drink lemonade to cool off, either. I'll bet Max is hot, too."

"I know!" said Valerie. "Why don't we get the hose and a tub and some soap? We could give Max and Peanut a bath. That should cool them off!"

"What a great idea," Hillary said. With that, the two friends gulped down the rest of their lemonade and went to collect the supplies they would need.

"There. We have all the stuff," said Hillary. "Now all we need are the dogs."

"I'll find Peanut, and you go home and get Max. I'll meet you back here," said Valerie.

Hillary hurried home, but before she could shout out, "Hi, Mom," she heard an angry voice coming from the living room. "I will thank you to keep that mangy mutt off my property and out of my flower beds. I am a quiet man, and all I ask is that I be left alone." Mr. Morgan almost knocked down Hillary as he stormed out the door.

Hillary walked into the living room. There she found her mother holding Max, who was covered with mud. "What happened, Mom?" Hillary asked.

"I'm afraid Max has gotten us into a bit of trouble with our neighbor," answered her mother. "He dug under the fence and got into Mr. Morgan's flowers. I'm afraid he ruined some of them."

"Oh, no," said Hillary. She took Max back to Valerie's house and gave him a bath. "I feel terrible about Max tearing up Mr. Morgan's flowers," she said.

"You should," said Valerie. "Now he'll really be out to get you."

"Maybe I can offer to plant some new flowers for him," Hillary said.

"But he said he wants to be left alone. I don't think he'd want you poking around in his garden," Valerie answered.

"There's got to be some way I can show him I'm sorry. I only want to be his friend," said Hillary.

That night at the supper table, Hillary didn't say much. "Why so quiet, Hillary?" asked her dad.

She told him what had happened with Max and Mr. Morgan and how she wanted to do something nice to show Mr. Morgan that she was sorry. "But I don't want to bother him and make him more angry," she said.

"Hmm. That is a tough problem," agreed Mr. Miller. "But I'm sure you'll come up with something. You've always been a very thoughtful person. Say, what's for dessert? Did you make some of your famous chocolate chip cookies today?"

"No, Dad. It was too— Hey! That's it!" shouted Hillary. "Mom, will you help me make some cookies tomorrow?"

The next morning, Hillary and her mother baked two batches of their famous chocolate chip cookies. They put some on a plate to give to Valerie's family, and they put some in their cookie jar. The rest they put in a metal tin like this one. (*Show tin.*) Hillary took the tin of cookies and put them on Mr. Morgan's front porch. Then she left.

Later that day, Hillary was trying to teach Max some tricks in her back yard. "Sit Max," she said, but Max kept trotting up to her to be petted.

"You'll never teach him to sit at that rate," came a voice from across the fence. It was Mr. Morgan. "Mind if I come over and show you how?"

"No," said Hillary.

So Mr. Morgan went through the gate into Hillary's yard. "You have to get Max to obey you and *then* you pet him. Like this." Mr.

Morgan commanded Max to sit. When Max obeyed, Mr. Morgan rewarded him with a pat on the back.

"I didn't know you knew anything about dogs," said Hillary.

"We had dogs the whole time my kids were growing up," said Mr. Morgan. "But our dogs never dug up the neighbors' flowers."

"I'm really sorry about that," said Hillary.

"And I'm sorry I haven't been a very good neighbor," said Mr. Morgan. "I guess I just spend so much time alone that sometimes I forget how to be friendly. And speaking of friends, would you like to have a cookie with me? A very nice friend of mine left some on my doorstep this morning."

"Yes, thank you," said Hillary. "Just let me go tell my mother."

The two new friends shared cookies in Mr. Morgan's back yard.

Jesus taught us that when we do something nice for someone, it is best to do it quietly, instead of bragging about our good deed. Somehow, being kind to others doesn't mean as much if we brag about what we've done.

Let's Pray. Dear God, help us to be nice to other people because we want to, not so we can get credit for it. Amen.

(You may want to give the children each a cookie as they leave.)

TWENTY-FIFTH SUNDAY AFTER
PENTECOST
Amos 5:18–24

Proper 27
Faithfulness

Rotten Apples

Props and Preparation Needed

A piece of fruit that looks perfect on the outside but is spoiled on the inside. You could carefully bruise an apple, or freeze and then thaw an orange

A good piece of the same kind of fruit

A knife and a cutting board

One good piece of fruit for each child (optional)

The Message

Good morning, everyone. I brought a beautiful, shiny red apple with me this morning. Doesn't it look good? (*Hold up piece of fruit.*) It looks delicious. I'll cut it up so we can each have a piece, okay? (*Cut the apple in half, making sure the rotten part is exposed.*)

Uck! Look at that! This apple is all bruised and rotten inside. It looked so good before I cut it, but I certainly wouldn't want to eat this apple, would you? Still, this apple can be useful. We can use it as an example for our story this morning.

There was a man of God who lived long ago—over seven hundred years before Jesus. The man's name was Amos, and he was a prophet.

God was very angry at the people of Israel and asked Amos to deliver a message to them. Many of the people brought offerings to God at the temple where they worshipped. They held long religious festivals, singing loud songs and saying long prayers. On the outside, these people looked like they loved God and obeyed God's law. But then the very next day, those same people were dishonest in their businesses. They cheated the poor to make themselves rich. They looked good on the outside by doing all the religious things they were supposed to do on the Sabbath, God's holy day. But the rest of the week they were rotten, just like the inside of this apple.

132

This made God angry, so God instructed Amos to tell the people of Israel what the Lord really wanted from them. What God wanted more than anything was for the people to treat each other with fairness and respect. God still wants us to treat each other with fairness and respect, not just on Sunday, but seven days a week.

If we act like we love God in church—by saying prayers, singing hymns, giving money, and listening to the minister—if we act like we love God in church but hurt God's people the rest of the time, then God knows we really didn't mean the church stuff. It was fake. We were pretending. Because if we really love God, then we will want to be kind and honest and fair to God's people.

God doesn't want us to be like this apple (*hold up rotten apple*) that looks good on the outside but is rotten under the skin. God wants us to be like this apple (*cut a good apple in half and hold up*), good inside and out.

Let's Pray. Dear God, help us to show our love for you in the way we live our lives every day. Amen.

(As the children leave, you may want to give each of them a good apple.)

TWENTY-SIXTH SUNDAY AFTER   Proper 28
PENTECOST   Making Use of God's Gifts
Matthew 25:14–30

This Little Light of Mine

Props Needed

A flat, hard surface (such as a tabletop or serving tray)
A votive candle
A glass jar that fits over the candle (with the label removed).
Place the candle on the tray or table with the jar next to it
Matches
A song leader
Piano or guitar accompaniment

The Message

Good morning, everyone! We're going to begin our time together today with a science experiment. You can see that I have a candle and a jar. First, I will light the candle. That's a nice, strong flame, isn't it? The candle is burning brightly. Now, what do you think would happen if we put this jar over the candle? Let's try it and see. (*Put the jar, upside-down, over the candle.*)

Look what's happening. The light is getting dim. Now the candle has gone out. When we covered the light with the jar, the candle went out. Does anyone know why that happened? (*Pause for answers.*) Right. Just as people need something in the air called oxygen to breathe and keep on living, fire—like the flame on this candle—needs oxygen to keep on burning. When we covered the candle with the jar, the candle could not get enough oxygen, so it went out.

God has given each of us a flame or a light. That is the light of God's love. Jesus taught the world about God's love by showing love in everything he did. He healed the sick, helped the poor, and made friends with those who had no friends. Jesus even died on the cross to show all of us how much God loves us. God wants us to share this love with others, too. Just like the candle and the jar, if we try to hide the love we've been given or keep it all to ourselves, it will die. But if we share the love of God with others, it will shine brightly and grow. What are some ways we can share God's love or let our lights shine? (*Pause for answers. Be prepared to 'prime the pump' with examples of your own.*)

There's a song about this that I'd like us to sing. It's called "This Little Light of Mine." If you know the song, help me teach it to the others, okay? That will be one way you can let your light shine. (*Teach song.*)

This little light of mine (*hold up right index finger*),
I'm gonna let it shine.
This little light of mine,
I'm gonna let it shine,
Let it shine, let it shine all the time.
Hide it under a bushel (*cup left hand over right index finger*),
No! (*Take left hand away quickly*)
I'm gonna let it shine.
Hide it under a bushel (*repeat hand movements*), No!
I'm gonna let it shine,
Let it shine, let is shine all the time.
Shine all over (*your town's name*)(*move index finger around in a circle, away from your body, then back in*)
I'm gonna let it shine.
Shine all over _____,
I'm gonna let it shine,
Let it shine, let it shine all the time!

That was very good! With all these lights shining, the world will certainly be a brighter place.

Let's Pray. Dear God, we thank you for the love you have given us. Help us to share that love with others, as Jesus taught, so that the whole world will shine brightly. In Jesus' name. Amen.

TWENTY-SEVENTH SUNDAY AFTER   Proper 29
PENTECOST   Sharing
Matthew 25:31–46

On Sharing

Prop Needed
A winter jacket

The Message
Good morning! Were you cold on your way to church this morning? This is the time of year when it starts to get really cold, isn't it? (*If this is not true in your area, adapt the story by talking about the cold weather in other parts of the country.*) I sure was glad I had this warm jacket to wear this morning. (*Hold up jacket.*) Today we're going to talk about a boy who had no coat and someone who shared with him.

This story is about a boy named Paul and his best friend, Ronnie. They lived on neighboring farms. Neither family had much money. Paul and his mother lived on his Uncle Ben's farm because Paul's father had died three years earlier. Ronnie had four brothers and sisters. They lived with their mother and father. There were a lot of people in the family, and the crops had not done very well for a couple of years. Plus, two of Ronnie's brothers had their tonsils taken out in the fall, which was expensive.

It was just about this time of year, in late November, when it started to get really cold. Paul had a beautiful new leather jacket to keep him warm. He had earned the money for it himself by doing extra chores all summer long for Uncle Ben. On that very cold day in late November Paul noticed that his friend Ronnie was wearing only a sweater and shivered all during recess.

Paul realized that Ronnie probably didn't have a jacket, so that afternoon he asked his mother if he could give his jacket from last year to Ronnie. "Sure," said Paul's mother. "I think it should fit him because you're a little bit bigger than Ronnie is."

Paul went to the closet and took out his old jacket. He looked at it carefully and saw that it looked pretty crummy—worse than he'd remembered. The lining was torn and the cuffs were frayed. Paul picked up both his old jacket and his new jacket and ran to Ronnie's house.

He knocked on the door. When Ronnie answered, Paul shoved the new leather jacket at him and said, "Here. This is for you."

"You can't give this to me," said Ronnie. "This is your brand new jacket that you earned yourself."

"I can so give it to you," Paul said. "It's mine to give, and I want you to have it. Now I gotta go help Uncle Ben. Bye." Paul turned and walked home, wearing his old, worn coat.

On the way home, Paul thought about what he'd done. He was truly glad he'd given Ronnie the better coat. He was a little worried about what his mother would say, though. When Paul got home, he and Uncle Ben finished the chores. Then they went inside to wash up for supper. His mother noticed the jacket he was wearing right away.

"Paul," she said, "I thought you were going to give that jacket to Ronnie."

"I gave him my leather one," Paul said. "I was too embarrassed to give him this one. I hope you're not mad."

"You earned the coat yourself, Paul. If you wanted to give it away, that was up to you," said Uncle Ben.

Just then the phone rang. Paul's mother listened for a few minutes and then said, "The jacket was Paul's to give. We hope Ronnie enjoys wearing it as much as Paul enjoyed giving it to him."

Paul's mother hung up the phone. Then she said, "I'm glad you wanted your gift to Ronnie to be nice, but what will you wear this winter?"

"Couldn't we find a less expensive one of some kind?" asked Paul. "It doesn't have to be leather, and I'll pay you back. I promise."

"Maybe we could look in the catalog after supper," said Uncle Ben.

They found a jacket they could afford. It wasn't as warm as the leather one, and Paul had to wear his collar turned up all winter, but he was never sorry that he had given his special jacket to Ronnie, and he never complained about being cold.

Jesus taught us that whenever we share what we have with someone in need, we are sharing with Jesus. Jesus knows the kind things we do for other people and is proud of us when we do them.

Let's Pray. Dear God, thank you for the many gifts you have given us. Help us to share generously with others. Amen.

Appendix

Appendix

How to Prepare Flannel-board Figures
  Cut the page containing the needed flannel-board figures out of the book. Glue the page onto a piece of stiff cardboard, such as the cardboard that comes with a new shirt. Cut around the outline of each figure. Color the figures, using crayons, marking pens, or colored pencils. Glue small squares of medium-grade sandpaper to the top, bottom, and middle of each figure.

3 Magi

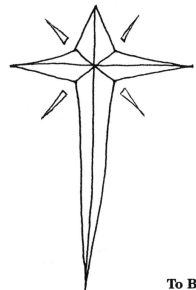

Bethlehem
Star

To Be Truly Wise
(pages 18–19)

143

Jerusalem

Manger

Chief Priests/Astrologers

Kneeling Magi

King Herod

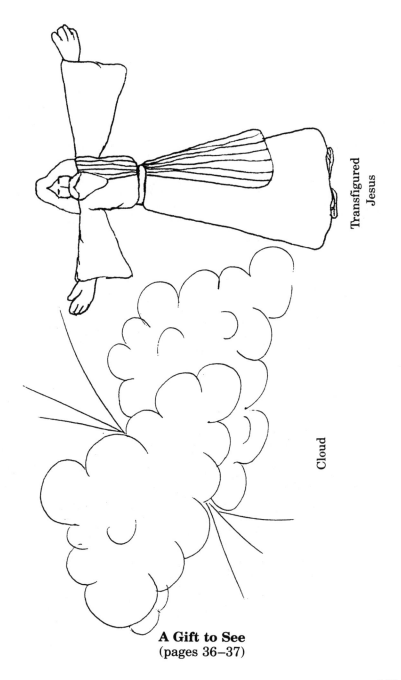

Transfigured
Jesus

Cloud

A Gift to See
(pages 36–37)

151

Mountain

153

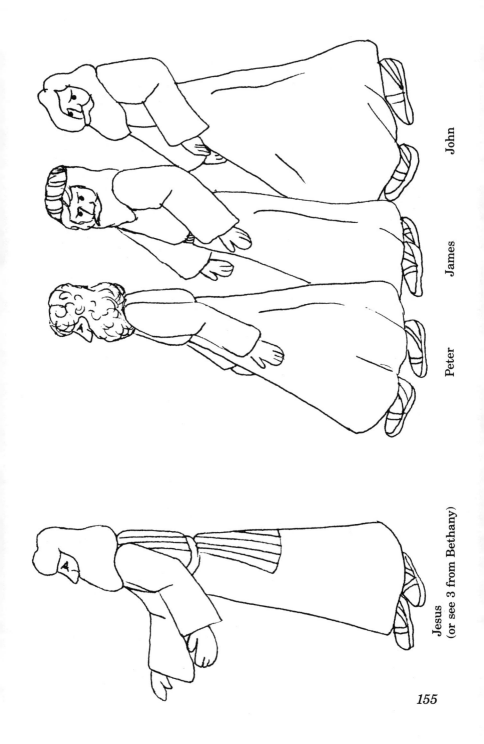

John

James

Peter

Jesus
(or see 3 from Bethany)

155

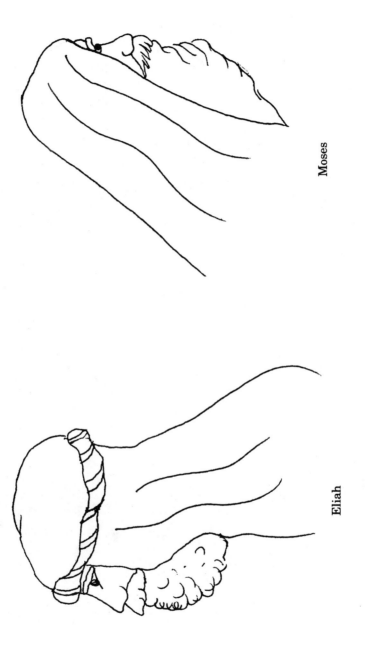

Moses

Eliah

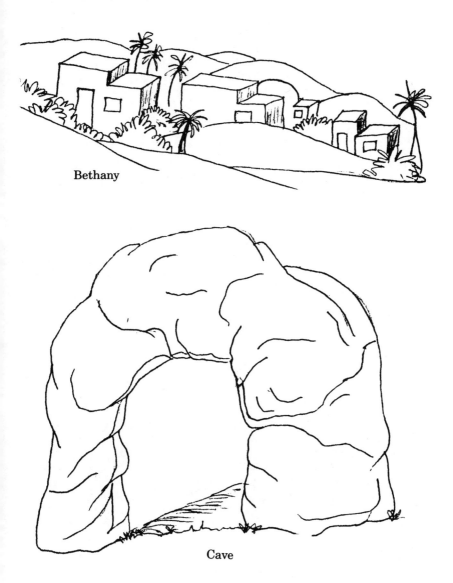

Bethany

Cave

Three from Bethany
(pages 48–49)

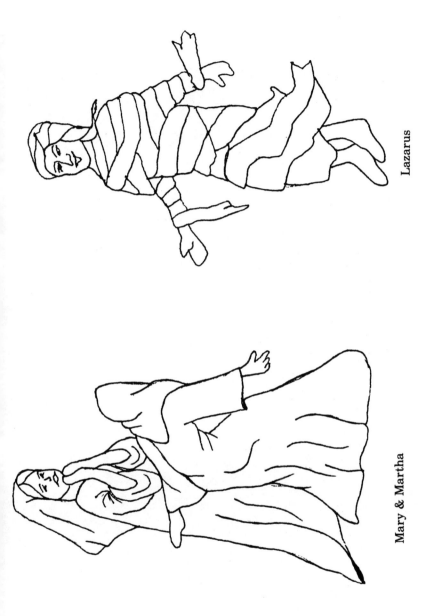

Lazarus

Mary & Martha

Disciples

163

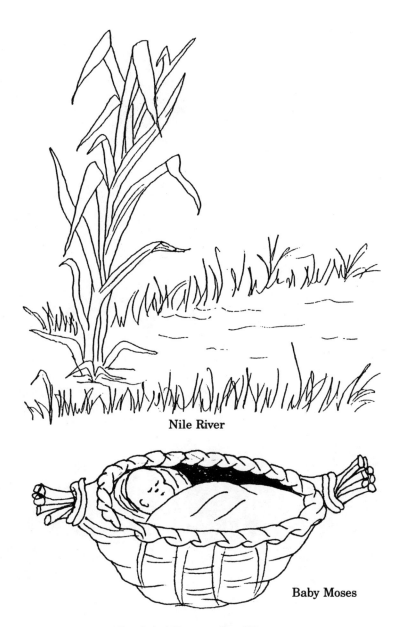

Nile River

Baby Moses

Cruisin' Down the River
(pages 86–87)

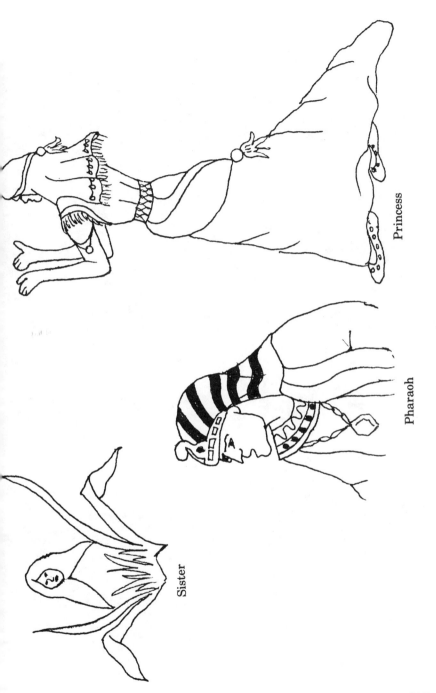

Princess

Pharaoh

Sister

167

Adult Moses
(or see Moses Revisited)

Troubleshooting
(pages 88–89)

Hebrew Slave/Egyptian Taskmaster

Hardworking Slaves

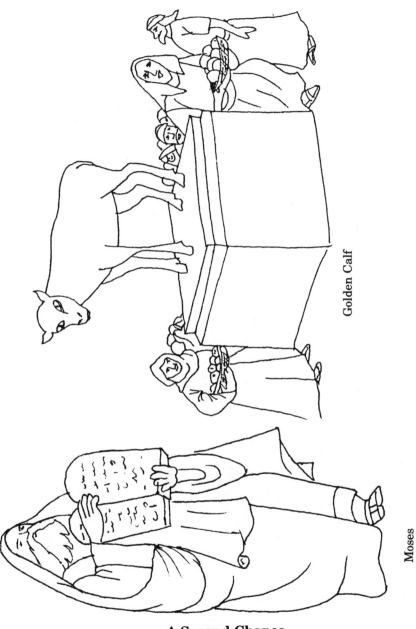

Golden Calf

Moses

A Second Chance
(pages 110–11)

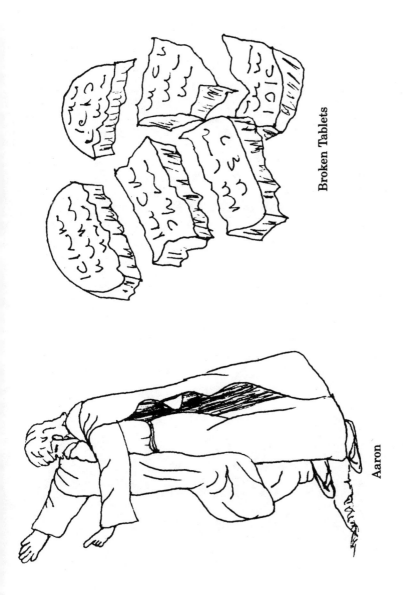

Broken Tablets

Aaron

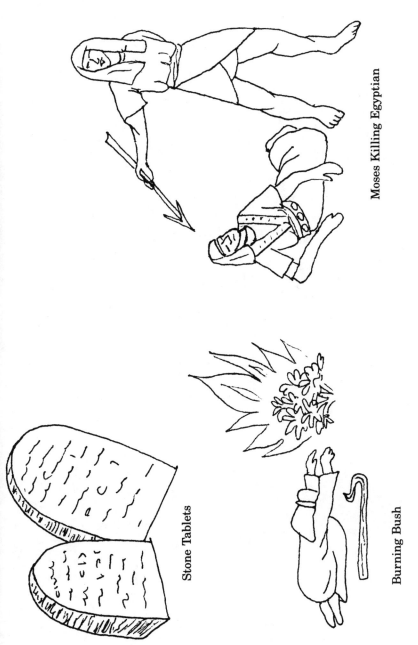

Moses Killing Egyptian

Stone Tablets

Burning Bush

Moses Revisited/Troubleshooting
(pages 118–19)

179

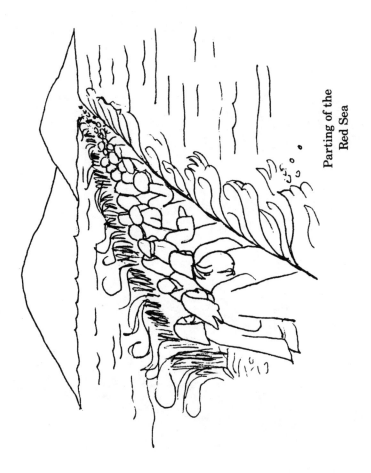

Parting of the
Red Sea

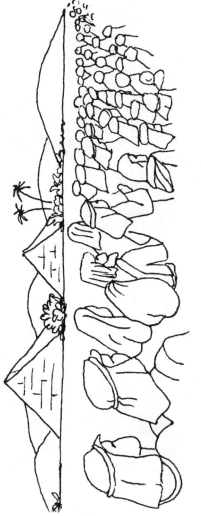

Hebrews in the Desert

How to Make the Flannel Board

Cut a piece of masonite or foam board to the desired size. Using powder-blue flannel four inches larger than the board (Diagram 1), pull the flannel to the back of the board, making sure it is smooth and taut on the front. Glue or tape the corners of the flannel to the back of the board first (Diagram 2). Then glue or tape the top and bottom edges (Diagram 3), and finally the side edges (Diagram 4).

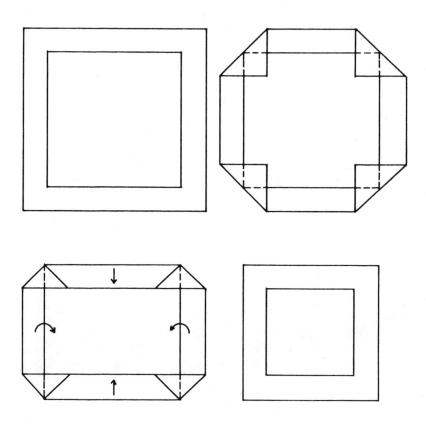

Indexes

Scripture Index

Topical Index